THE POWER OF YOUR SENSORY-SELF

Discover the Secret to a Stress-Free Life
Using the Power of Your Senses

JUDI M. WOLANSKY, OTA/L

EVAN DANIEL MEDIA
New Providence, New Jersey

Published by **Evan Daniel Media**
New Providence, New Jersey

For information about permission to reproduce sections from this book or for special discounts for bulk purchases, please contact Sensory Authority at **www.SensoryAuthority.com**

Disclaimer: This book is intended as general information only, and should not be used to diagnose or treat any medical condition. Due to the specific nature of health problems, this book is intended to supplement, not replace, the advice of a trained medical professional. You are advised to consult with your doctor before adopting any of the suggestions in this book, as well as about any condition that may require diagnosis or medical attention. The author and publisher disclaim any liability arising directly or indirectly from the use of this book. The activities in this book are intended to offer information of a general nature to help you in your quest for emotional, physical, and spiritual well-being. They are not a replacement for professional therapy.

Cover Design by Michael Rehder
Interior Design by KUHN Design Group

Printed in the United States of America

ISBN: 978-1-7356766-0-9 (print)

Library of Congress Cataloging-in-Publication-Data:
Wolansky, Judi
The Power of Your Sensory-Self/Judi M Wolansky.
p. cm.
1. SEL000000 - Self-Help 2. SEL036000 -Self-Help Anxieties and Phobias.
3. SEL024000 - Self-Help Stress Management.

Library of Congress Control Number:
2020920911

This book is dedicated to Danny,
and every person who has ever suffered
from stress, anxiety, and depression

LIFE-CHANGING MOMENT
Is this Book for You?

Do you long to increase your self-confidence, joy, and sense of fulfillment? Do you desire to gain control over stressful situations so you can live a more meaningful, purpose-driven life? Then this book is for you!

The information contained in this book unveils the mystery of how sensory experiences (encounters that stimulate the senses) directly affect the quality of your life. The sensory-centered exercises are uniquely designed to help you understand how your interpretation of sensory information impacts your temperament, behavior, and self-image. This knowledge will increase your sensory awareness and reveal the secret to living a stress-free life.

Sensory experiences have formed your understanding of life since the day you were born. For example, the comfort of being held in your parent's arms helped ease the transition from the dark, warm, quiet climate of your mother's womb to the bright, cold, loud atmosphere of this world. From your very first day of life, you were beginning to learn that certain sensory encounters produce anxiety, while others reduce stress.

You quickly found comfort through a multitude of sensory interactions. The comforting touch of a soft blanket, a gentle caress, or being snuggled made you feel safe and loved. Equally soothing were sights to behold, like faces, colors, shapes, and patterns, or movement that included rocking, swinging, or bouncing. Tranquility was found through the sound of soft-spoken words or a soothing lullaby. Other sensory events also helped reduce your anxiety and stress, such as the deep pressure created by a hug or a heavy blanket, the oral stimulation from a pacifier or bottle, and the familiar scent of your mother, father, or home. Sensory experiences comforted you when you were young, and they will continue to do so throughout your lifetime.

This sensory education will guide you through the process of discovering the sensory events that produce feel-good chemicals in your brain. These chemicals are the ones that make you feel happy and content. It will also teach you to identify and modify the sensory encounters that stimulate cortisol production, the chemical that increases stress and anxiety. I guarantee this knowledge will increase your self-esteem, improve your mood, and empower you to live your best life ever!

POINT TO PONDER...

Every day you will face challenges and situations that cause stress and anxiety. These experiences flood the brain with cortisol, affecting your heart rate, temperament, and behaviors. So how is it possible to enjoy a stress-free life?

You can reduce anxiety and manage stress by learning how to optimize brain chemistry. This book will teach you how you can increase the feel-good chemicals in your brain and reduce the stress-producing ones by using the untapped power of your senses.

CONTENTS

THE STORY THAT STARTED THIS MISSION

Several years ago, I met a young man named Danny, who had been battling a drug addiction for many years. Danny was a likable person who desperately longed for a different life. Upon listening to him speak, I wondered how and why a kind person like this, who had the support of a loving family, ever started using drugs in the first place, so I asked him. His simple, honest response inspired the creation of this life-changing program.

Danny stood before me with a fixed, upward gaze, as he nervously pushed his wavy blond hair from his eyes. Then, standing ever so still, it appeared his mind had drifted back in time so he could adequately prepare his response. I quickly realized that my simple question had unearthed years of pain. His body was motionless as beads of sweat formed on his brow, then his eyes filled with tears. A look of fear and confusion swept over his face, and his voice quivered as he began to speak.

Danny explained that outwardly, people could not see that he was a very nervous and anxious person. He said that he silently suffered from the pain of anxiety, an anguish that made him feel different, and as if he did not fit in. He said that this pain was relentless, and he did not know how to lessen it or make it stop.

With his mind still fixed deep in his past, he shook his head as he questioned why, in a society that teaches people to just say 'no' to drugs, hadn't anyone taught him what he was supposed to say 'yes' to when he felt lost and hopeless. As he lowered his head, he sorrowfully uttered, "That's when I started using drugs. I wanted to stop the pain." Danny ended this moment by saying, *"You know, people worry when kids struggle with their schoolwork, yet schoolwork won't kill you, but anxiety, now that can kill you."*

He then looked my direction, yearning for a response, but I was speechless. I knew he was right. Strategies for managing anxiety and stress are not taught in schools. Many practical skills needed to be successful in life have been overlooked for years. This pivotal moment inspired this mission to teach people how they can use sensory strategies to manage their anxiety, so they can enjoy the successful, happy life they deserve.

Danny helped me design the Life Changers Sensory Solutions Program by candidly sharing his life experiences. I am thrilled to report that Danny now enjoys a life of sobriety. He learned how to manage his stress using sensory strategies, and he has surrounded himself with a supportive community. Danny also found help to overcome his addiction at *Any Length Retreat* in Austin, Texas.

A Message from The Author

I can assure you that by reading this book, you have embarked on a journey to improve your life. As you start your sensory education, I feel it's important for you to know a little bit about me and my professional experience. My name is Judi Wolansky. My husband and I live in New Jersey, where we raised our three children.

Throughout the years, I have provided occupational therapy services to clients in various settings, but my passion is working with children and young adults. I thoroughly enjoy interacting with clients and their families to help them achieve their goals.

Occupational therapy (OT) is a fascinating profession. It originated as a holistic method of caring for the mentally ill. Since then, it has evolved into a profession that offers a variety of services for people of all ages and backgrounds. Occupational therapists use creative techniques to help people develop the skills they need for participation in their daily occupations, with occupations referring to activities that *occupy* a person's time. This includes self-care activities, care of others, education, work, hobbies, and social skills.

In treating clients, I use a sensory-based approach. Many occupational therapists use this method and find it incredibly effective. This technique includes creating sensory routines and modifications that help clients improve their skills. I found remarkable success using sensory strategies, but after meeting with Danny, I started to wonder if I had been treating the symptoms and not the root cause of an individual's problems. Danny's words made me question what role anxiety played on a client's abilities and performance. It also caused me to reflect on the importance of treating anxiety when providing services.

This reflection prompted me to adapt my treatment style. I now address a client's anxiety with sensory strategies before focusing on their skill development. I introduced various sensory inputs, knowing what works for one client may not work for another. I was shocked to discover that these children and young adults could easily achieve success in other areas when given strategies to quell their anxiety. There were also noticeable improvements in their self-confidence and social participation. The results were utterly amazing. These clinical observations revealed how anxiety stifles people's abilities and affects their lives. It also confirmed that sensory strategies are incredibly effective in reducing stress and anxiety.

This book was created to share this life-changing information with you. I have seen people's lives changed dramatically by using sensory strategies, and I am confident that this knowledge will change your life too.

Although the information contained in this book reflects on services provided in professional settings, it is not intended to replace professional evaluation and care.

Anxiety…An Unseen Assailant

Anxiety was the catalyst that led to Danny's addiction because he could not find any way to stop his pain. Today, many people are suffering from anxiety. Anxiety can be overwhelming. It is often the root cause of low self-esteem, isolation, depression, and self-injurious behaviors. It impacts every aspect of a person's life, yet it is often minimized, stigmatized, or misunderstood. The time has come for this to change.

This book will teach you how to overcome anxiety and manage stress in your life. The strategies introduced in this program are grounded in the cutting-edge science that correlates a person's sensory processing ability with their actions. This sensory education reveals how each encounter that stimulates your senses affects your brain chemistry. Some of these encounters will activate the feel-good chemicals in your brain that make you feel happy and capable, while others increase the chemicals that make you feel anxious. Learning to identify the sensory encounters that contribute to your stress will allow you to avoid them, and knowing how to distinguish them from the ones that soothe you will empower you to overcome anxiety.

HOW TO USE THIS BOOK

This book begins by introducing each of the senses, followed by discussions on how sensory events influence behaviors. It is based on research by the esteemed occupational therapist and clinical psychologist, Dr. Jean Ayres, who studied the correlation between sensory processing and human behavior. The first section of this book provides an overview of how your nervous system processes information received through your senses, and how your ability to tolerate sensory events shapes your life. You will quickly discover that although some sensory encounters increase stress, many more can be used to reduce it.

The second section offers an in-depth education about each of your amazing senses. It will teach you how each sense impacts your life. This journey of discovery will reveal little known facts about the senses and their effect on your perceptions, performance, self-image, and behaviors. This insight is truly enlightening!

The last section of this book contains the Life Changers Sensory Solutions Program. This easy-to-use program allows you to enjoy the benefits of sensory therapy from the comfort of your home. Each of the twelve sessions includes therapeutic activities that teach you how to use sensory strategies to improve all areas of your life. The sessions include detailed instructions to guide you through each exercise and are designed to be self-administered or used in a group setting. I would encourage you to complete one session per day to simulate the format of professional services.

Optimal results are achieved when the exercises are implemented as instructed. I strongly encourage you to write out your answers, as opposed to merely thinking about them. Studies show that documenting responses increases the rate of a program's success by nearly fifty percent. It also increases your attention to detail to heighten your sensory awareness, which is the goal of this program.

Therapists and counselors have found extraordinary success when using the Life Changers Sensory Solutions Program, and I am thrilled to make it available to you today. If you would like to learn more about sensory processing and how it affects your behaviors, I encourage you to visit our website at **www.sensoryauthority.com**.

Please visit **http://www.SensoryAuthority.com/reader-bonus** to download additional copies of the therapeutic exercises contained in this book.

HOW OUR SENSES SHAPE OUR LIVES

CHAPTER 1

INTRODUCTION TO THE WORLD OF SENSORY

I'm curious, my friend, how did this book come into your life? Do you want to learn more about sensory integration, how you receive, regulate, and organize sensations? Or perhaps you desire to learn more about yourself and how this wonderful world of sensory experiences affects your perceptions, engagement, and behaviors?

Whatever led you to this book, I feel confident you will be forever changed by its content. You will become more assertive and empowered as you become acquainted with your unique 'sensory-self.'

This book teaches you how the nervous system processes sensory events and how your unique processing pattern alters the production of feel-good chemicals in your brain. You will also discover how specific sensory encounters are contributing to your stress. This knowledge will help you understand your own behavior, as well as the behavior of others.

This sensory education teaches you how to incorporate your sensory preferences into activities to make them more harmonious and pleasurable. This includes pursuits in work, recreation, and social gatherings. You will also learn how to develop your sensory awareness so you can identify the encounters that contribute to anxiety.

Sensory-centered solutions will also be discussed for those occasions when you are placed in a stressful environment. This will prepare you to establish a personalized sensory action plan that will enable you to enjoy the fulfilling, productive life you deserve.

Through my experience of providing sensory-based therapy, I have witnessed amazing transformations when clients learn how to use sensory strategies to improve their lives. This knowledge enables them to control stressors and reduce anxiety. It also helps them feel more confident and productive.

Sensory awareness benefits people of all ages. It empowers people to take control of their lives by managing stressors that cause anxiety, frustration, or rage. It also helps increase a person's self-confidence, productivity, and success. I have witnessed many people's lives changed by this extraordinary program, which is why I feel honored to share it with you today.

Life-Changing Moment...

MY STORY

It was that time again when report cards were sent home. My three older sisters smiled as my parents viewed their nearly perfect grades. Then the dreaded moment came when I had to show them mine.

I knew it would be a disappointment, though my parents never seemed to view it that way. They would encourage me, reminding me that I had obtained a perfect score on the New Jersey standardized test and recorded a higher than average IQ score when tested. Yet, those results did little to ease the embarrassment and pain I felt each day. The disparity between my grades and IQ was puzzling, not only to my parents and teachers, but also to myself.

I had convinced myself that I was just not that smart. Furthermore, I lacked physical coordination and was often one of the last kids to be picked when teams were formed in gym class. Since I smiled all the time and was known for being kind, my peers would signal apologies to me to soften the blow. To avoid humiliation when tests were handed back or when teams were picked, I learned to use humor as a diversion. My quick wit earned me the title of class clown. You see, class clowns are not always born; some are made.

As the years passed, I tried to hide the anxiety and depression caused by my challenges. Music became my refuge once I discovered I could carry a tune. Humor and music were now my two best friends, but by this time, I had lost confidence in myself and had withdrawn from others. It was a very lonely and painful time in my life. And along with everyone else, I wondered: what was wrong with me?

Things began to change during my last year of high school. A concerned teacher asked me what I was thinking about during his class. I told him that

I thought how hard it was to sit still because I needed to move, and how the sounds behind me were distracting. I also explained that I felt a need to see everything that was going on: in the classroom or the hallway. He suggested that I should stand or move about in the back of the room for future classes.

This idea changed everything because I was able to satisfy my sensory needs and focus on class instruction. I was so grateful for this teacher's help, but I believed this revelation had come too late. I was already fully persuaded that I was neither smart nor athletic and that my future was bleak. Yet, over time, I started to learn more about sensory imbalances and how they impact people's lives, and this awareness changed my life.

I went on to enroll in college and graduated—at the top of my class. I then built a successful career in occupational therapy, specializing in sensory integration for children, who often remind me of my younger self. And today, I devote my time to educating people about sensory processing so they can also enjoy the successful life they deserve!

Our Sensational World

We live in an extraordinary world of sensory experiences. For example, a relaxing day at the beach includes sand caressing our feet as we gaze upon the expansive sky reflected in the boundless sea. The sound of the waves crashing on the shore is enhanced by the scent of the salty air floating on a summer breeze that gently sweeps the hair from our eyes. The bright, majestic sun's penetrating warmth envelops us like a blanket, so we sip an ice-cold drink, longing to satisfy our seemingly unquenchable thirst.

This repertoire of sensory encounters affirms that our senses are vital for processing events in our life. Throughout our lives, sensory experiences have been our best teacher. We learned to speak by listening, felt comforted by touch, determined what was safe to eat by smelling and tasting, and learned about colors, faces, and more, through our eyes. These same senses taught us that sharp to the touch is dangerous, or the smell of smoke means fire.

Senses have the unique ability to create joyful moments or alert us to potential danger. *Isn't it perplexing that we have desired to learn more about our physical abilities through fitness programs and our cognitive skills through brain-building programs but overlooked the importance of learning about our sensory system, which impacts every area of our life?*

Individuals each have a unique ability to process information received through their senses, just as each person has their unique physical and cognitive abilities. It is important for people to understand that each person experiences a sensory event differently.

For some people, the sand at the beach might feel like sharp shards of glass, and the sun's warmth could be stifling. The sound of the waves could go unnoticed by some or be too loud for others. How people perceive these sensory events will affect their mood and how they behave when at the beach.

If these sensory experiences were perceived as pleasant, an individual would be calm and happy. If these sensations were perceived as offensive, a person would appear frustrated or agitated. This explains why my perception of sensory encounters in school differed from many of my peers. A lot of the sensory events in school were hard for me to process. This affected my engagement, performance, and, most importantly, my self-esteem.

I suspect that a lack of education regarding sensory processing may be a contributing factor to many problematic situations in life, including the child who misbehaves, throws tantrums, or is failing in school. It may also be the reason why some people are uncomfortable in social settings or unable to hold a job. Perhaps people who are aggressive and quick to anger might also be reacting to a sensory overload or imbalance. Offensive sensory events in an environment will increase a person's anxiety, leading to these types of behaviors. Sensory intolerance has also been shown to be a contributing factor in depression, substance abuse, and self-harm.

POINT TO PONDER...

Through years of working with clients; I realized that misbehaviors could be corrected when a person is given the necessary sensory input to balance and meet their needs. A balanced sensory system also helps people to be more attentive, productive, and successful.

Life-Changing Moment...

SINCE THE DAY WE WERE BORN

Since the day we were born, our senses have played a unique role in our development and perception of life. From infancy, we learned to do things by watching others. We discovered that looking at patterns and colors were soothing, and we turned our gaze away from things that were scary.

As children, we were calmed by a soft, reassuring voice and learned our language by listening to others speak. We relaxed when listening to soothing music or a familiar children's song. When frightened by a loud noise, we sought solace in our parents' loving arms, knowing that their touch would comfort us.

We also explored the world by touching things. We learned that soft items are pleasant, hard objects can hurt us, and sharp objects are dangerous. Our sense of smell was also hard at work. We were comforted by the familiar scent of our home, parents, or favorite blanket. From the day we entered the world, sensory experiences helped shape our lives.

When we cried, we were comforted by our mother, who stroked our face to wipe the tears from our eyes. To help us feel calm, we were swaddled tightly in a blanket that gave deep pressure (proprioceptive input), and we sucked on a pacifier (oral stimulation) to reduce anxiety. We learned how to cope and handle life's many stressors by using different sensory experiences.

Sensory experiences have been our greatest teacher and comforter since the day we were born. Learning how sensory encounters affect our lives is the key to success. The information in this book will unveil the extraordinary power of this sensational world so you can enjoy a happy, stress-free life!

What Calms You Down?

Now that we identified some of the sensory encounters that were used to comfort you when you were young, I would like you to take a moment to determine what strategies you currently use to soothe yourself when feeling anxious or angry. This is not as easy of a task as one might assume. Most people are not consciously aware of the tactics they employ to manage their stress.

I am confident that upon completing this program, you will be able to identify a multitude of strategies that will help you manage stressors.

This is the goal of this program. It is designed to increase your awareness and understanding about sensory encounters so that you can reap the full benefit of every sense.

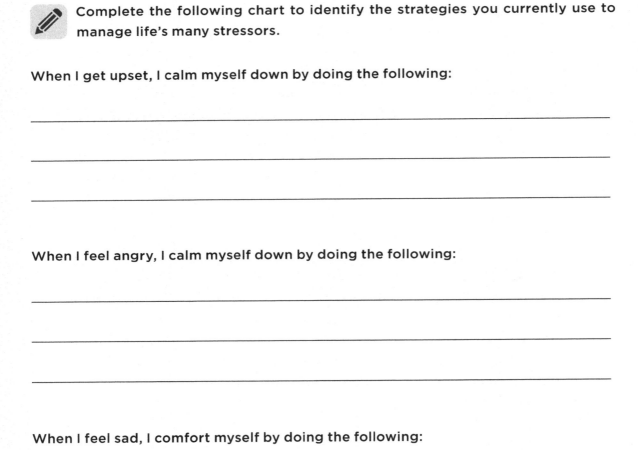

Complete the following chart to identify the strategies you currently use to manage life's many stressors.

When I get upset, I calm myself down by doing the following:

_____

_____

_____

When I feel angry, I calm myself down by doing the following:

_____

_____

_____

When I feel sad, I comfort myself by doing the following:

_____

_____

_____

POINT TO PONDER...

Why do some people stomp their feet, clench their fists, or tense their muscles when they are angry? Perhaps people do these things because these activities provide a deep pressure input that stimulates the proprioceptive sense. Proprioception is not often mentioned when discussing our senses; however, this sense is responsible for detecting our body position and regulating our muscle strength. It also plays a crucial role in making us feel secure and calm. This explains why a weighted blanket or deep massage is so comforting. They stimulate the receptors in this system, heightening our body awareness and making us feel secure and calm. As you continue reading, you will learn more life-changing facts about your senses and the different ways they affect your life.

CHAPTER 2

WHAT IS SENSORY PROCESSING?

Sensory processing describes how the nervous system receives and organizes information gathered from the senses. The brain is continually receiving messages from each of the senses. It then processes and interprets this data to determine the appropriate physical or emotional response. If the brain determines that a sound is too loud, it may prompt you to cover your ears. If it perceives the volume to be too low, it will direct you to increase the volume. How a sensory event is perceived directly impacts a person's behaviors.

In the past, sensory processing and its effect on stress had not been given much attention. Most sensory books limit their discussions to the effects that sensory processing disorders have on children. You will find that this book is entirely different. This book is designed to teach people of all ages how their ability to receive and process information gathered from the senses is impacting their lives.

It is important to remember that each person has a unique threshold for tolerating a sensory event. How a person's nervous system receives and interprets the sensory input will impact how they react to it. For example, let's say that you witnessed a child running full speed into a sliding glass door. You saw and heard their little body smash into the glass, and you gasped—anticipating their cry from the pain. But instead, this child stood up and continued playing without making a sound or rubbing their head. Children who respond this way are often referred to as being 'so tough.' Next, you see a child who barely bumps into a chair while playing. This benign encounter caused the child to cry in pain. Children who respond this way are frequently scolded for 'acting like a baby.' Observers might also believe this child is over-reacting, but what if they were not? What if it was their nervous system that was over-reacting to the information received through their senses?

We all tend to base our assumptions of how one should respond to situations on how we might react. This is an unreliable measure as we all process sensory stimuli differently. We do not expect other people to exhibit the same strength or athleticism as we do; therefore, we should not expect them to react to sensory information in the same way either.

One way to better understand why the first child under-responded and the second child over-responded is to recall a time when a friend jokingly punched you in the arm. You may not have paid much attention to a few gentle whacks on the arm, but you would certainly react if your friend fired off a rapid series of forceful blows. You would feel pain that would cause you to react. These punches are similar to how neurons (nerve signals) send signals to the brain to construct our responses.

The first child who did not experience pain has an under-reactive nervous system. His nervous system transmits pain signals up to the brain, slowly and sluggishly—similar to getting one or two blows on your arm. The second child who cried from pain has an over-reactive nervous system. His neurons fired rapidly, repeatedly sending the pain signal to the brain. This is like being punched in the arm over and over again. This example illustrates how sensory processing abilities vary from one person to another and how the interpretation of a sensory event affects a person's behavior, self-image, and social reputation. This analogy can also be used to help us understand other behaviors.

Let us consider why some babies cry much more than others. They may cry because sounds are too loud, lights are too bright, or a gentle touch feels like a smack. Or perhaps they are crying because of a vestibular intolerance that causes them to feel dizzy when lifted. Unfortunately, infants are unable to communicate what they are feeling. Parents must experiment and try various approaches to calm them until finding one that works, though they may not understand why it was effective. These babies are in distress because they are suffering from a sensory imbalance.

Like babies, adults will often lack the skills to adequately identify what is upsetting them or why they behaved in a particular way. For example, why do some people hum or whistle throughout the day? What causes them to make noise continually? Do they crave auditory input, so they create sounds? Or do their own sounds dampen extraneous noises that are too much for them to process? Another reason may be that the vibration created by their humming stimulates their tactile and vestibular system, which is soothing to them. These examples illustrate that we subconsciously satisfy our sensory needs through our behaviors.

We can all relate to having avoided or craved a particular sensory experience at one time or another. For example, when I was young, I hated to wear socks or snug-fitting clothes because they caused me pain. I was also bothered by the intense odors like burning leaves or paint because these smells made me nauseous. Therefore, I avoided these uncomfortable sensory experiences. However, I did enjoy the touch of a soft blanket, the sound of music playing, and the freedom to move around. This prompted me to seek out these pleasurable experiences.

These sensory requirements impacted my education, self-image, and social engagement during my youth and some of my sensory preferences have lingered well into my adult years. As I learned more about sensory processing, it became easier for me to identify which sensory events were calming and which ones contributed to my stress.

Sensory likes and dislikes may not always be so readily discernable. Developing sensory awareness skills and assessing your sensory processing abilities will take some time, but the investment of your time will surely be worth it. As you continue reading, you will begin your journey of discovering your sensory-self so you can enjoy a more productive, fulfilled, peaceful life.

POINT TO PONDER...

Sensory Processing Disorder (SPD) is a neurological condition that makes it difficult for a person to adequately receive, interpret, and respond to certain sensory inputs. A person must meet specific criteria of impairment in order to receive this diagnosis.

Although the information in this book discusses processing patterns and behaviors, it is not suggesting that the uniqueness of a sensory processing style resulted from a disorder. On the contrary, this book teaches that each person has a unique ability to process information received through the senses and how their brain interprets this data affects their behavior and shapes their lives.

If you would like more information about Sensory Processing Disorders and corresponding behaviors, I encourage you to visit **www.sensoryauthority.com**. There you will find detailed information about SPD, along with educational materials, blogs, and sensory product information.

Some Like It Hot

Most of us recognize that we each have our own unique sensory preferences. This prompts the phrase, 'Some like it hot, and some like it cold.' Sometimes the impact that sensory experiences have on our lives is undervalued. For example, for you, a fun day might include a large group of friends, loud music, and dancing. However, your partner may prefer more sedentary activities with fewer friends in a quiet environment.

You may also savor the aroma of essential oils and the taste of spicy foods, but your partner may feel these odors and flavors are repulsive.

The difference in the sensory preferences listed above seem obvious when noted for comparison, but how often are you exposed to sensory encounters that are unsettling to you? How many times have you questioned the impact that these encounters have on your life?

Sensory encounters shape our lives. They either increase or decrease anxiety. They can help us to wake up or help us to relax. Although most of us fail to recognize how sensory imbalances affect our lives, it is important to understand that too much or too little sensory input can increase our stress, anxiety, and decrease our self-worth. These encounters also influence our temperament, productivity, and relationships.

For a moment, imagine how you would feel if you lived in the quiet, scent-free environment that your partner preferred—one where you sat around with only a few friends. Now consider how your partner would feel living in a loud, scent-filled environment surrounded by lots of friends actively moving around. Situations where our sensory needs are not met create stress. They make us feel agitated, frustrated, and anxious. This is why it's important for you to learn about your sensory system and how it shapes your life. This knowledge will empower you to reduce anxiety and control stressors in your life. It will help you modify your environments and alter how you socialize so you can succeed in all areas of your life.

CHAPTER 3

OVERVIEW OF THE NERVOUS SYSTEM

POINT TO PONDER...

People have always desired to learn more about physical fitness and the benefits of maintaining a nutritious diet. Undeniably, these topics are important, and there are countless books written on these subjects. This book aims to teach people about sensory processing, which is equally as important as physical and nutritional health. Sensory encounters teach, protect, comfort, and energize us. They also affect our physical and cognitive performance, and our behaviors. To fully appreciate how sensory encounters are received and processed, it is helpful to understand how the nervous system works.

We are all familiar with the five senses: the ability to see, hear, smell, taste, and touch. Although these senses are easily identified, the role they play in our lives has only recently garnered attention. We also have other senses that affect our behaviors, though we are mostly unaware of them. Although every sensory encounter is processed through the nervous system, it seems many people have a vague understanding of how the nervous system works.

To better understand how the nervous system operates, we need to acquaint ourselves with this network's structure and dynamics. This is necessary to fully appreciate the power of your sensory-self. Since most of us are not familiar with this vast network's components, the descriptions have been simplified, and the key terms *highlighted* to make this tutorial easier to understand.

Every time one of our senses is exposed to an input, like sight, sound, smells, taste, touch, or movement, it stimulates the sensory receptors in our nervous system. The receptor receives information and sends it up to the brain to be processed and interpreted. The brain then generates a message that instructs us on how to react. Please note: Sensory information travels up to the brain, and motor messages (how to respond) travel down to our body.

The human nervous system is made up of two main parts: The *Central Nervous System* (CNS) and the *Peripheral Nervous System* (PNS). The *central nervous system* includes the brain and spinal cord, which is why it is referred to as the body's command center. The *peripheral nervous system* is the network of nerves that extends from the brain and spinal cord to connect the body to the *central nervous system*.

The nervous system works by receiving information through the peripheral nervous system (nerves) and sending that data to the central nervous system (brain) for interpretation. For example, the CNS determines if a touch detected by the PNS felt like a punch or like someone gently tapping your arm to get your attention. The way your brain interprets the touch will determine how you should respond.

POINT TO PONDER...

One way to envision how the nervous system operates is to compare it to dining at a restaurant. The waiter (a sensory receptor) receives your order (a sensory input) and sends it to the chef (the brain) through a series of staffers (neurotransmission). Once the chef (brain) receives the message, the order is processed and organized (sensory processing). The chef (brain) then sends the meal out to fulfill the order (the response). When the order is received and filled accurately, everything is working as planned (a balanced nervous system).

However, if something in this process does not work as expected, the chef (brain) might initiate an alternate plan, like offering the patrons free dessert to keep them satisfied. This illustrates how our brain prompts us to behave in a particular way to balance our nervous system and keep us satisfied. For example, the brain might prompt us to use our hands to shield the sun from our eyes or to cover our nose if we detect a noxious odor. This analogy should help you better understand how we receive, process, interpret and respond to information received through our senses.

What Is A Neuron?

Neurons are specialized nerve cells. They carry messages throughout the body. They transmit information to the brain for interpretation and communicate signals from the brain to the body. Neurons are remarkably busy. They can have as many as 15,000 connections with other neurons at the same time.

There are many kinds of neurons, and each is categorized by function. *Sensory neurons* send sensory signals up to the brain, and *motor neurons* carry action signals down from the brain. *Sensory neurons* receive data from both the environment and internal organs. *Motor neurons* respond by sending information down to the muscles, glands, or organs to elicit action.

How Do Neurons Communicate?

Most *neurons* never touch each other. They communicate by sending specific chemicals called *neurotransmitters* over the *synapse*, which is the gap that separates them. The short finger-like projections that extend from the *neuron* are called *dendrites*. The *dendrites* receive the chemical signal from the previous *neuron* and convert it into an electrical impulse. The signal is transmitted to the *cell body*, where it is processed. It is then transmitted out the *axon*, a long fiber that extends from the *cell body* to the *axon terminals*, which are located at the end. When the electrical impulse reaches the *axon terminal*, it initiates the release of the *neurotransmitters* that will carry the message over the gap to be received by the next *neuron's dendrites*. *Neurotransmission* continues, sending information up and down nerve pathways and throughout the nervous system at incredible speeds. Over 100 billion *neurons* give the brain this amazing processing power.

POINT TO PONDER...

Another way to understand how neurons communicate messages in our body is to compare this process to a cell phone call. When a call is initiated, it sends the call signal to the nearest appropriate cell phone tower. There it is processed and sent over the gap to the next tower. This is similar to how a sensory encounter (sight, sound, smell, taste, touch, or movement) transmits messages to the brain by sending a signal from one neuron to the next. The dendrites receive the sensory signal. The signal is then processed and transmitted over the gap to the next neuron. This sequence repeats itself until the message reaches the brain.

Similarly, a cell phone tower receives radio wave signals and transmits that signal from tower to tower until the call reaches its destination. Now suppose the tower delays or drops the phone signal, the call cannot be completed. This is comparable to how we experience problems with receiving and processing sensory information. Communication signals are sometimes delayed or lost in the process, affecting the result.

Neurotransmitters: Messengers of the Nervous System

Neurotransmitters play an integral role in communicating messages throughout the body. Everything we do, our thoughts, emotions, behavior, and motor skills result from neurotransmission. Neurotransmitters also regulate functions such as attention, concentration, memory, energy, sleep, mood, pleasure, anger, fear, and pain by activating neurons in specific parts of the brain.

There are several different types of neurotransmitters in our body, but we will limit the discussion to those that affect our mood, stress, and happiness. *Dopamine, serotonin, endorphins, norepinephrine,* and *oxytocin* are neurotransmitters that help us feel good. We can increase the level of feel-good neurotransmitters through activities like exercising, walking, being outdoors, music, and even by taking a shower. Sunlight, goal achievement, and human touch also increase these chemicals in the brain.

Norepinephrine happens to be different than the other feel-good chemicals because it can also act as a stress hormone. *Norepinephrine* is the neurotransmitter that enables us to react quickly as part of our fight or flight mechanism, which is activated when something threatens our safety.

Hormones, like *cortisol* and *adrenaline*, also act as neurotransmitters. They transport messages through the bloodstream, affecting our mood, behavior, and ability to manage stress. *Cortisol* provides health benefits when the level is balanced. It can help lower blood pressure and reduce inflammation in our body, but increased levels produce stress. We can reduce the *cortisol* level by getting a good night's sleep, and through activities such as meditation, praying, interacting with others, exercise, creative arts, laughing, and playing with pets.

Adrenaline, also called *epinephrine*, is the neurotransmitter responsible for arousal, attention, and energy. It causes our heart to beat faster, which increases the blood flow to our muscles to help us react in dangerous situations. Too much *adrenaline* produces acute stress, anxiety, and depression. Sensory enriched activities, like exercising, yoga, baking, gardening, and cycling, are just some examples of how we can lower the level of these stress hormones. Meditation, journaling, volunteering, and giving can also decrease levels, along with aromatherapy, music, various spices in foods, and interactions with others.

Glutamate and *GABA (Gamma-Amino Butyric Acid)* are the most abundant neurotransmitters in the central nervous system, and they each have opposing roles. *Glutamate* works like a gas pedal to activate nerve cell communication, and *GABA* serves as the brake to reduce or stop it. These are the dominant neurotransmitters used in neural connections. More than half of all the synapses release *glutamate* to excite nerve cells, and *GABA* to reduce cell activity. *GABA* calms down an overstimulated system. It also helps with our vision, sleep, and motor control, in addition to reducing anxiety. Activities like yoga or tai chi can help increase levels of GABA.

Neurotransmitters are responsible for creating our happiness or increasing our stress. We can learn how to increase the level of feel-good chemicals in our brain by identifying the sensory inputs that bring us joy. We can also learn how to decrease the levels of neurotransmitters that make us feel anxious by avoiding inputs that increase stress.

As you continue reading, you will learn how to recognize the sensory experiences that increase the feel-good chemicals in the brain and those that produce cortisol. This awareness will help you to manage stressors in your life.

If you would like to learn more about neurotransmitters, please visit **www. SensoryAuthority.com**. There you will find information about the effects of having too much or too little of a particular neurotransmitter.

How Substance Abuse Affects the Brain

Diet, stress, medications, and medical conditions can impact our bodies' communication system. They affect the transmission and reception of neurotransmitters. This breakdown in communication explains why our behaviors may change when we are stressed or taking medications.

Also, drugs linked to substance abuse have a significant impact on this process. They increase the levels of some neurotransmitters while suppressing the transmission of others. Unfortunately, this unnatural process destroys receptors, which rewires the brain. These drugs damage the nervous system, rendering it unable to create that 'feel good' sensation from natural inputs.

Damaged receptors are what lead to the pattern of addiction.

Higher doses of drugs are required to create a 'high,' but eventually, even the drugs will not have the ability to replicate these intense feelings. This causes the user to increase their dose, which can lead to a life-threatening overdose.

POINT TO PONDER...

Studies have found that over time, receptors that have been damaged by drug abuse will begin to repair themselves. This is called neuroplasticity, which means the brain's ability to change and heal. These findings revealed that after one year of sobriety, the brain's structure and function showed signs of improvement. This allows the individual to once again experience pleasure from naturally occurring events.

Life-Changing Moment...

A MAN, A BAT, AND A BALL

I first witnessed the power of neuroplasticity during a clinical rotation at a skilled nursing facility. I was tasked with designing a therapeutic activity to promote functional improvement for a client named Mr. D. He was a tall, frail man in his mid-seventies who had to use a wheelchair because of Parkinson's Disease. His upper body slumped forward because it was hard for him to sit up due to muscle weakness, and he rarely spoke a word.

I noticed that Mr. D had posters of baseball players in his room, so I asked him if he had ever played. He quietly uttered, 'hit the ball.' This was yet another devastating symptom of his disease: his brain's communication signals were disrupted by the disease, affecting his speech pattern and voice. He could only whisper about three words at a time.

The following day, I brought in a foam-covered baseball bat that came with a T-stand. I knelt beside Mr. D and showed him the bat. His hand trembled as he stroked the bat, and tears filled his eyes. As he held the bat, his posture started to improve. This was very encouraging.

I set-up the T-stand in the rec hall, and with assistance from my co-workers, Mr. D was able to stand with the bat in his hand. He looked so happy that I could hardly contain my excitement as he started to swing the bat, but he abruptly stopped before hitting the ball. Mr. D looked sad, and I was confused. Each time he would swing the bat, he would stop before contacting the ball. My supervisor then explained that Parkinson's Disease had affected the circuitry in the brain. The communication between neurons was now impaired, and he was not able to complete the task. My heart sank. I could not imagine what it must have been like for Mr. D. It was such a sad moment.

Later that week, when I returned for my shift, the supervisor ran to greet me and said, "You're never going to believe it. Wait until you see." Mr. D was then wheeled into that same hall and handed the bat. I was instructed to pitch the ball to him while he remained seated. He aimed and hit the ball clear across the room. It was a miracle! I pitched to him for almost an hour, and he hit all but three balls. I was overjoyed!

Excitedly, Mr. D told me how Joe DiMaggio played for the Yankees and Jackie Robinson for the Dodgers. My supervisor exclaimed, "Oh my gosh, that's incredible." I agreed, acknowledging his outstanding batting skills. She corrected me and explained that she was not talking about his athleticism, but about his ability to speak in full sentences. She said that he had not done so in the five years he lived at this facility. This was yet another miracle!

I was amazed. I could not believe how much had changed since the first time we tried this activity. My supervisor then explained why there was such a vast improvement in his ability to participate. She said that because Mr. D. did not play T-ball, he had never created a neural pathway in his brain to hit a ball off a T-stand. Therefore, he stopped midway through the activity the first time I tried it with him. She then said, "But he did play baseball, so when the ball was pitched to him, the familiar activity stimulated previously established neural pathways in his brain so he could complete the task."

She turned and said, "Now that is the power of neuroplasticity. The brain has the ability to modify connections and rewire itself." She added that this activity had not only stimulated the neural connections for Mr. D to hit the ball, but it also stimulated the connections for him to speak about his favorite sport. Then she turned to walk away but ended by saying, "The brain is fascinating, and there is so much more to learn about the power of neuroplasticity."

POINT TO PONDER...

Sensory therapy uses sensory strategies to reawaken neural pathways that have been impacted by illness or injury. This demonstrates the vital role that sensory events have in shaping our lives. The more you learn about sensory processing, the more you will appreciate the power of your senses.

Neuroplasticity: The Brain's Ability to Change

Neuroplasticity is a scientific term used to explain how nerve connections in the brain can develop and change. *Developmental neuroplasticity* means we create new neural pathways from experience and learning. *Injury-induced plasticity* means the brain can adapt and change paths that have been obstructed by injury or illness.

One way to visualize this process is to picture a roadway that includes several bridges to reach its destination. The 'road' represents the neurons, and the 'bridges' represent the neurotransmitters that bridge the gaps. If an incident occurred that impeded traffic flow on that road, an alternate route would be established to keep traffic flowing. This is similar to how the brain re-routes connections that were affected by illness or injury. The neurons are able to reorganize and create an alternate route of neural communication.

Developmental plasticity begins at birth and continues throughout our lifetime. Neural connections are established from learning and exposure to sensory events. During this time, neurons sprout more branches (dendrites). Repeated exposure to sensory events helps us to develop and reinforce neural connections that make processing more efficient. Connections reinforced by sensory stimulation become stronger, while the ones that are not reinforced will weaken. Over time, many of the connections that are not used are eliminated through a process called *synaptic pruning*. This pruning results in an efficient system of neural communication.

POINT TO PONDER...

One of the best ways to understand neuroplasticity is to think about a time when you created a path through the woods. The first time you walked through the forest, you had to step on branches and leaves to create a path. If you traveled this same path repeatedly, the borders would become more apparent. This is similar to neuroplasticity: repeated exposure to sensory encounters establishes an efficient pathway in the brain.

Now, if a tree fell and blocked the path you had established, you would create a new one by bypassing the obstruction. This is similar to how the brain creates a new path of communication when the original path becomes obstructed by illness or injury.

CHAPTER 4

IT MAKES
SENSE TO ME

We are sensitive beings who process life through our senses in a world that provides a wide array of sensory experiences. Our ability to see, hear, smell, taste, and touch allow us to enjoy all that life has to offer. Each one of our senses holds a specific responsibility for collecting and processing sensory information. Although each of our senses has a unique role and function, they do not work in isolation. On the contrary, all our senses integrate to form our perception of events and situations. They are like pieces of a puzzle that join together to form a picture.

Sadly, most people know little about the five external senses of the human body. They know that sight is received through the eyes, sound through the ears, smell through the nose, taste through the mouth, and touch through the skin. However, they do not understand how sensory experiences impact their brain chemistry and behaviors.

Recently, researchers have focused their study on 'hidden' senses and their contribution to sensory integration. These include the vestibular, proprioceptive, and interoceptive systems. The vestibular system is responsible for detecting our balance, while the proprioceptive system detects the position of each body part. The interoceptive system is responsible for detecting and regulating our inner senses, such as sleep, hunger, body temperature, and other important senses. These senses are discussed in greater detail throughout the book. However, it is crucial to recognize that they are as valuable as our external senses.

Sensory and Survival

The sensory system not only provides us with information about our world; it is also vital to our survival. We are alerted to danger by things like sounds, noxious odors, soured foods, and our protective sense of touch. In addition to protecting us, our sensory system is also responsible for teaching us. We learn by watching others, hearing the spoken language, and by feeling things. And let us not forget that this system plays a fundamental role in creating moments of pleasure like the smell of dinner cooking, a gentle touch that provides comfort, or the sound of music.

Sensory Coding

How sensory information is presented to us is called sensory coding. Sensory coding has a significant impact on our perception of a situation. The intensity, frequency, and duration of our exposure to a sensory event help to determine how we interpret the situation. This explains why too much of a preferred sensation can morph into an offensive one.

The significance of sensory experiences in our lives is immeasurable. These experiences started the moment we were born, and they undoubtedly impact every aspect of our lives. Wouldn't you agree that it is time to learn as much as you can about the sensory system, and how it shapes your success, behaviors, and happiness?

Sensory Terminology

Several terms are used throughout this book that may be new to you. Please take a moment to familiarize yourself with the following terminology:

Senses: Our ability to see, hear, smell, taste, touch, balance, move, and internally regulate.

Neural: Nerves related to the nervous system.

Sensation: The awareness of stimuli from the senses.

Sensory: Information received by any of our senses.

Sensory System: Includes sensory receptors, neurons, neural pathways, and parts of the brain.

Sensory Processing: How the brain receives and interprets incoming messages from our senses to generate the appropriate motor (movement) and behavioral (action or conduct) response.

Sensory Integration: The process of how we receive, organize, and interpret sensory stimuli from all senses.

Sensory Balance: The precise amount of sensory input to satisfy our needs.

Sensory Overload: Too much of a sensory input, overwhelming the nervous system.

Sensory Retreat: To distance yourself from sensory inputs to give your nervous system time to rest.

Sensory experience, sensory event, sensory information, sensory input, sensory data, sensory exposure, sensory interaction, and sensory situation refer to interactions with sensory stimuli. These terms are used interchangeably throughout the book.

Individualized Sensory Needs

When teaching families about sensory processing, I find it best to use stories about everyday experiences that most people can relate to and understand. These depictions emphasize that everyone processes sensory information in their own way. These stories help to explain how too much of a sensory input, like lights that are too bright or sounds that are too loud, can be overwhelming. When there is too much or too little of a sensory input, it affects a person's mood or behaviors. These analogies also help to explain how too little input, like dim lights, the volume being too low, or not getting enough movement, can increase anxiety. The key to success is maintaining the proper balance of sensory information in your daily life.

Let us consider how differently people behave on a chilly day. Some people may wear a heavy winter coat, others a light jacket, while some may be comfortable wearing only a long sleeve shirt. Each person has a unique tolerance of the temperature and will dress accordingly to feel satisfied by balancing their sensory system. This is true for all our senses, including how close we stand to others or how we season our foods. We feel most content when the amount of sensory input is 'just right.'

POINT TO PONDER...

If people have different requirements to maintain their temperature regulation, isn't it conceivable that we each have unique requirements to regulate our other sensory systems?

Sensory Sensitivities

Although I use relatable stories to explain how sensory processing affects a person's behaviors, it is sometimes hard for people to fully understand a sensitivity if they have not experienced it themselves. For example, I had a 7-year-old patient who only spoke in a whisper. It seemed to most that he was timid, or there was a physiological explanation for his quiet voice. During one of his sessions, I noticed that he winced when other children spoke. I asked him if the sound of their voice hurt his ears, and he whispered, "Yes."

In meeting with his family, I discovered that he watched TV with the volume so low that others could barely hear it. He would also cover his ears for no apparent reason when he was in the kitchen. I asked him if the hum from the refrigerator and dishwasher were too loud for him to tolerate. He again answered, "Yes." I then asked him if he thought he was whispering when he spoke. He quietly replied, "No, it sounds like I'm shouting."

His responses indicated that he has an over-sensitive auditory system that made it hard for him to tolerate sounds that most of us filter from our hearing, like the sound of appliances or running water. Even his quiet voice was too loud for him. Although the severity of his sensitivity is uncommon, auditory sensitivities are not.

Many people have an over-sensitive auditory system that makes it hard for them to filter out or tolerate certain sounds. The distracting or unpleasant noise may not be obvious, but it can be a contributing factor to anxiety. Therefore, it is important to recognize that everyday sensory events, like common background noises, can trigger stress.

Sensory processing directs people's behaviors. The person who hums or makes sounds throughout the day may do so to satisfy their sensory craving. This also helps them create a 'white noise' that masks other sounds. People who roughhouse are seeking deep pressure to balance their nervous system, and individuals who bite on pen caps or fingernails do so to satisfy their need for oral stimulation. These sensory-directed behaviors are no different than eating when hungry or sleeping when tired. Our behaviors regulate our nervous system by fulfilling our sensory needs.

When you crave or avoid a particular sensory experience, your brain is prompting you to balance your nervous system. During the times when you are exposed to too much or too little sensory input, your anxiety increases. Thankfully, there are several products available today to help people regulate sensory information. For example, the boy who could not tolerate noise was given noise-canceling headphones, headbands, and earplugs. These helped to reduce his anxiety by giving him control over sounds.

Sensory Imbalances are a Distraction

How can too much or too little sensory input impact your behavior? Imagine it is a cold, blustery, winter day, and you run outside without your coat to get the mail. Unexpectedly, your neighbor, who is wearing a heavy winter coat, stops to speak with you. Initially, you are able to concentrate on what he was saying, but after a few minutes, you become distracted by thoughts of getting warm. When the conversation ends, you rush inside to warm up. Your spouse asks you what the neighbor wanted. Your reply is brief and uninformative, "I don't know, something about snow removal." Then you emphatically proclaim, "It's freezing out there!" Clearly, you were more focused on the sensory distraction that you were to the conversation. This example illustrates how sensory imbalances become a distraction, impacting a person's actions and ability to process information.

This is quite similar to the child who cannot

remember what they learned in school because they were too distracted by their own sensory imbalance. They may have been distracted by sounds, a need for visual input, or a need to move around. These children can easily recall what other students were wearing, saying, or doing during class because they were distracted by activities that satisfied their sensory needs.

Sensory imbalances affect people of all ages. These distractions impact productivity in the workplace or school. An irritating buzzing noise from a computer, lights that are too bright, an offensive odor from a co-worker's seafood salad, or something as trivial as popcorn stuck between your teeth can be distracting. These distractions affect a person's executive functions, such as memory, sequencing, planning, and emotional regulation. They impede a person's ability to achieve success, and they increase anxiety. This is why you need to learn about sensory processing and how to identify sensory imbalances. This sensory education will teach you how to recognize and control these distractions so you can enjoy a successful, fulfilling, happy life.

POINT TO PONDER...

Have you ever found yourself distracted by the sound of other people talking when you were trying to read or do paperwork? These noises do not only impede productivity, but they can also alter your mood by making you feel annoyed, frustrated, and stressed. Interestingly, some people are equally distracted by silence. These are the people who need to hear sounds to feel secure. Isn't it fascinating that each person has their own sensory preference to feel content?

Sensory Coding: Intensity, Frequency, and Duration

We have all heard the repetitive beep from an alarm clock. It is a disturbing noise that repeats over and over again. If the person who set that alarm fails to silence it, the volume (intensity) of the repeated beeps (frequency) and the length of time it continues (duration) can irritate others who hear it. However, if the alarm is quickly silenced, the sound will have been noticeable, but not irritating. It is the combination of intensity, frequency, and duration of a sensory encounter that forms our perception of the experience.

We can all understand how someone's level of frustration would intensify from a continuous, irritating noise. The sound of a car alarm is a good example: once it is triggered, it continually beeps until the owner turns it off. This annoyance can affect your mood, behavior, and stress level, depending on the sound's intensity, frequency, and duration. This is yet another example of how everyday sensory experiences contribute to stress.

Today, most classrooms use fluorescent lights as the primary source of illumination. If a person is light sensitive, spending several hours a day (duration) under bright lights (intensity) may cause eye strain, fatigue, and a headache. If the person was in the classroom for a short time, it might be tolerable; however, if they were exposed to those bright lights day after day (frequency), they may feel exhausted and stressed.

It's conceivable that a person would attribute these negative feelings as a disdain for school, when, in fact, that is not the case—it was a sensory overload that caused them to feel stressed and fatigued. Sensory imbalances can also occur in social or professional environments, impacting our perception and temperament. This is yet another reason why people should learn about sensory needs, preferences, and challenges.

Our Senses Work Together

We often isolate our sensory likes or dislikes when referencing sensory encounters, yet the neural systems are not independent of each other. They collectively work together to create our interpretation of a sensory experience.

Imagine you are outside on a bright, beautiful day watching a college football game when suddenly you hear a loud, powerful, booming sound. Cheering fans jump to their feet, and the band begins to play. You quickly realize that the powerful blast came from the cannon that is used to signify that the home team scored. These sights and sounds intensified the excitement of the game.

Now imagine you are outside gazing up at the stars on a beautiful night. Suddenly you hear a loud, powerful, booming sound; only this time, you feel anxious and concerned. The information from your other senses sends you a message that forms a vastly different perception of that sound. It is the totality of sensory information from each of our senses that determines how we perceive an event and how we should respond.

This comparison demonstrates how our perception of the loud sound differed in each environment. Sometimes, we fail to recognize how one sense impacts another. For example, odors can influence what we see, and sights can influence what we hear, and so on.

Interestingly, a research study that used brain imaging revealed that if we see a rose while smelling it, our brain processes the scent differently than if we were to look at an image of something with a toxic odor while smelling that rose. Studies also found that the taste of food is affected by what we hear when eating it. These findings should heighten your curiosity about how sensory experiences are shaping your behavior and your life.

You can begin to increase your sensory awareness by actively noticing what you hear, see, smell, or feel when you go places or do things.

For example, when you eat dinner, what are you looking at, what odors do you smell, and how does the chair you are sitting in feel? Is the environment too quiet or too loud? Some of these things may be irritating if dining at home, but tolerable when dining out. This indicates that the context and environment influence our perception and tolerance of a sensory experience.

Calming, Arousing, or Organizing

Sensory encounters can affect us in a variety of ways. Some are calming and help us relax while others are alerting and energize us. There are also times when a sensory experience can have both a calming and arousing effect on our nervous system.

When we receive the amount of sensory input deemed 'just right,' the nervous system is balanced. This helps us organize our thinking and increases our attention, concentration, and comprehension. For instance, when you jump into a pool on a hot summer day, the water is initially arousing. However, after a few minutes, the deep pressure from the water makes you feel calm. This combination of stimulating and calming your nervous system helps organize your thoughts. Other types of sensory encounters can also have a similar effect.

We know that listening to invigorating music produces a cortical charge in the brain that arouses the nervous system. If you are feeling fatigued or having difficulty organizing your thoughts, listen to a few upbeat songs. This can make you feel more alert and focused. You could also splash cold water on your face or use other sensory activities to excite your nervous system.

What Do You Do to Energize Yourself?

By now, you should be starting to recognize how sensory encounters shape your life. You learned how sensory experiences were used to comfort you when you were young, and earlier, you identified the strategies that you are currently using to manage your stress. Identifying calming methods is extremely important; however, it is equally crucial to pinpoint the ones that make you feel more alert.

For the next activity, you will document the strategies you currently use to make yourself feel more alert and focused. Again, this task is not as easy as one might assume. When asked how people energize themselves, they frequently state that they rely on caffeine or sugar. Perhaps they do not realize that sensory encounters can also be used to arouse the nervous system.

Please complete the following statement, listing the strategies you currently use to energize your nervous system.

To make myself more alert and energized, I do the following:

_____   _____

_____   _____

_____   _____

POINT TO PONDER...

Have you ever sat down for a period of time and started to feel drowsy? This is quite common, but next time, before you reach for caffeine or sugar, try listening to a few upbeat songs. Invigorating music produces a cortical charge in your brain. You will also find that walking, eating sour foods, drinking carbonated beverages, and smelling specific scents can also be used to energize you. These are just a few examples of the various sensory encounters that can arouse the nervous system. You will learn more strategies and understand why they work as you continue reading.

Brain Preparedness

People understand that stretching before exercising prepares their muscles for a workout; however, they may not realize that doing an organizational task before an assignment can help prepare the brain for their activity. It is important to recognize that every sensory encounter will have an effect on your nervous system. This knowledge is vital for learning how to use sensory strategies to organize your thoughts and increase your productivity. The importance of managing our thoughts is undervalued. However, everything we do requires the ability to conceptualize and sequence actions in our minds before we can execute them. This is why it is important to learn how sensory encounters affect our executive functions because when our thoughts are organized, it allows for efficient, productive thinking.

Have you ever made a shopping list for the grocery store? As you create the list, you organize the items according to the layout of your supermarket. When you review the list immediately before entering the store, your mind is prepared. You know where to begin, and you map out the steps that follow. Brain preparedness increases your efficiency and productivity.

In therapy, I teach clients how to use organizational exercises before completing a task. The organizational activity does not have to be related to their actual assignment; however, something as simple as sorting coins or alphabetizing a short list of words will prepare the brain for organizational tasks. You should try an organizational activity before your next big presentation or project. It helps prepare the mind and reduce anxiety.

What Is A Sensory Diet?

A sensory diet is an action plan that indicates various ways a person can maintain a balanced nervous system. It is not much different than a personalized workout routine that lists exercises to work each muscle group, only the sensory diet lists activities that reduce stress and anxiety. Occupational therapists are skilled at creating sensory diets for children. These 'diets' help clients regulate their emotions by eliminating stressors and providing sensory encounters that satisfy their nervous system. They also

help the child to focus and attend. Adults can also benefit from identifying sensory encounters that improve their lives. You will soon have the opportunity to create your own sensory diet in the therapeutic application section of this book.

Sensory Integration

Sensory integration is how we receive, organize, interpret, and modulate information from our body's senses to produce an appropriate, purposeful response. The nervous system is responsible for coordinating the information from our senses. It then interprets this data to direct our movements and behaviors.

Nature and nurture each play a vital role in the development of the sensory system. Recurrent sensory interactions strengthen neural pathways. This helps us to modulate various sensory stimuli. A well-balanced sensory system then enables us to participate in daily activities and social exchanges appropriately.

Sensory integration allows us to do things like shift our body to the appropriate spot on the tennis court so we can swing our arm in a particular area to make contact with a ball that our eyes were fervently tracking. The sound of the ball striking the racket, in addition to the pressure, force, and vibration, communicates to our brain the totality of this experience. This scenario describes how our actions require feedback from several senses. A person's ability to integrate this sensory information is what creates their precision and skill.

Sensory integration that functions as intended is like a well-oiled machine: everything works flawlessly. It is not much different than a car. If the system is calibrated, it provides you with safe, efficient transportation. However, if that car had a faulty gas pedal, or worse yet, a defective braking system: it would alter the vehicle's performance. This is similar to how an imbalanced sensory system can affect a person's performance and skills. So why is it that we have not learned much about sensory integration in the past?

A Sensory Revolution

The importance of sensory awareness is beginning to gain the recognition it deserves. Places like restaurants, malls, and NFL stadiums have added sensory rooms because research indicates that overwhelming sensory encounters increase stress and affect a person's emotional regulation. These sensory retreats benefit children and adults alike. Several schools now offer alternate seating options, provide movement breaks, and have replaced detention with mindfulness and yoga.

Progressive corporations have also recognized the benefits of utilizing sensory modalities. Many companies now offer a variety of options to help employees balance their nervous system. These sensory rooms, sensory retreats, and enrichment programs help reduce stress, improve employee retention, and increase productivity.

Sensory awareness does not only improve our lives; it helps us to understand other people's behaviors. It helps us appreciate why a co-worker asks peers to be quiet or why someone slams a door or drawer shut. It also explains why one person turns off the bright overhead lights, and why another saturates themselves in perfume.

Life-Changing Moment...

THE MISUNDERSTOOD CHILD

I vividly remember his first day at therapy: the adorable four-year-old boy hid his face as his tearful mother spoke of his challenges. Like most parents I meet, his mother was distraught and overwhelmed.

The young boy accompanied me into the play gym, looking down as we walked. His little face offered no smile, though the words he spoke were genuine and informative. As he ran around and stumbled over the gym equipment, he told me how his teacher told him he was 'bad' and 'crazy.' Shocked by his words; I wondered why any teacher would teach a child such terrible things about themselves.

It was evident that this little fellow had trouble staying still. He needed to move, and his under-sensitive vestibular system affected his balance and coordination. He also made unusual noises and felt the need to touch anything that piqued his interest. Frequent reminders to 'pay attention' or 'be careful' embarrassed him, causing him to apologize for his actions.

Most of us can understand how his behaviors would be frustrating to his teacher, but many of us fail to recognize how his actions affected him. He wanted to focus on his work and succeed. He longed to fit in with his peers, but his impaired sensory system prompted him to do things to satisfy his sensory needs.

His overwhelming desire to move, touch things, and make sounds, along with his postural instability, indicated a child with a sensory processing disorder. Children with this disorder have difficulty modulating and integrating sensory information. Thankfully, after several weeks of sensory-based therapy, this young boy started to flourish. His progress continued as he and his mother came to understand his sensory needs.

Months later, I had the opportunity to meet this boy's father. Steeped in emotion, his father shared how life at home used to be stressful. He said that his son's challenges led to marital distress because he and his wife would argue over how they should handle their son's behaviors. He stated that things are now much better since they learned about sensory processing. This awareness changed everything for them. Then as tears filled his eyes, he asked, "What happens when families don't learn about sensory processing? What will happen to their child?"

CHAPTER 5

YOUR SENSORY SELF

POINT TO PONDER...

People will often refer to a person as being overly sensitive or insensitive. These are general comments that usually refer to a person's emotional state and not their ability to process sensory stimuli. It is important to understand that each of our senses is processed uniquely. One system may be over-sensitive, and another may be under-sensitive. Therefore, generalizations are not accurate when describing a person's sensory processing ability.

When we think of our senses, we usually think of the part of the body that receives input and its function rather than the intricate way our central nervous system processes incoming sensory information from each of those senses. Sensory processing is quite fascinating, and it is undeniably life changing. There is so much to learn about each of the senses and how they can increase or reduce stress. The following chapters contain an overview of senses so you can fully appreciate the role they have in your life. This will give you an in-depth understanding of how your nervous system receives and processes information and how your individualized sensory processing ability affects your life.

Processing impairments in children are also included in the discussion. This helps you recognize the sensory processing areas that were challenging for you when you were young and the effect they had on your life. They may have impacted your behaviors, academic performance, social acceptance, and your self-image. The more you learn about sensory processing and its role in creating your success or failures, the easier it will be to understand and accept yourself. This information will also help parents, teachers, and therapists understand why a child behaves in a particular manner.

When discussing sensory processing, we must always consider the intensity or the amount of the sensory input a person needs to feel content. For example, picture a room that has one large window on a bright sunny day. Imagine that the window has a room darkening shade attached to the top. When the shade is fully opened, it allows an abundance of sunshine to illuminate the room; however, some people in the room may feel the room is too dark with the shade open, so they turn on the lights. These are people who require a lot of visual input because they have an under-sensitive visual system.

Others in the room may feel it is too bright, so they turn off the light and lower the shade to the window's mid-section. Now they think the amount of light in the room is 'just right.' Their visual system is not particularly over nor under-sensitive to input.

Still, another person may feel the room is too bright, even with the shade partially closed. They may lower the shade leaving only an inch of the window exposed. These people have an over-sensitive visual system. It only takes a small amount of input for them to feel satisfied.

This analogy should help you visualize how varying amounts of sensory information can affect each person differently. This insight is a starting point for understanding how sensory encounters shape your behaviors and your life.

Life-Changing Moment...

HOW CONTROL AFFECTS STRESS

Years ago, I saw a doctor on TV discussing stress. He explained that stress intensifies when we lack control in a situation. He said that the less power we have, the more we will experience stress.

At that time, I was a stay-at-home mother to three young children. Simple tasks like showering or cooking had become stressful because the children were continually in my care. I could not safely watch all of them while doing these activities.

I quickly realized that this doctor was right; it was not my little ones that caused the stress; it was the lack of control of my situation. The children needed constant attention and care. Over the years, his words stayed with me, and I often shared his wisdom with others because we sometimes mis-identify the root cause of our frustration.

I have since learned that his theory about control is also true for managing sensory encounters. The ability to control the intensity, frequency, and dura-tion of a sensory input creates our overall sensory experience. For example, we may tolerate the sound of the TV when we control the volume; but if some-one else is manning the remote, we may have less tolerance for the noise. This also holds true for other sensory experiences, and it may explain why some people like to give a hug, but they do not want to be hugged.

As adults, we have some degree of autonomy over sensory inputs. We can move away from a chair that wobbles or feels uncomfortable. We can also turn off the lights or change our clothes if they are bothering us.

Unfortunately, children do not have this freedom. They are expected to sit in a hard chair at school, wear the clothes that were purchased for them, and tolerate hugs from relatives. These sensory encounters may overwhelm the child, but if they were given some control in the situations, it might increase their ability to tolerate these sensory inputs.

Recently, I heard a lecture by a well-known doctor who studies sensory pro-cessing. She suggested that if a child has difficulty tolerating clothes, we should let them dress themselves. If they cannot tolerate water touching their skin, we should let them hold the shower head to control the water. She also suggested that if a child is unable to tolerate a particular sound, we should record the noise and encourage the child to listen to it, giving them control of the volume. This helps increase their tolerance to the sound. Her advice confirmed what the doc-tor on TV had stated years earlier: lack of control intensifies stress.

A, B, C's of Processing Patterns

Perhaps you can relate to some of the behaviors associated with a particular sensory processing pat-tern. They may remind you of yourself or a fam-ily member, coworker, or friend. Four processing patterns are used to categorize the behavioral pat-terns associated with an over or under-sensitive system. To help you better understand the four sen-sory processing patterns, I have organized the cat-egories in alphabetical order: A is for Avoider, B is for Bystander, C is for Craver, and D is for Detector.

- *Avoiders* have an over-sensitive system. This causes them to avoid sensory encounters that they cannot tolerate.

- *Bystanders* have an under-sensitive system. They do not easily detect a sensory input and may require external cueing to recognize it.

- *Cravers* also have an under-sensitive system, but their system prompts them to seek more input to process the sensory experience.

- *Detectors* have an over-sensitive system. They notice or detect even the most subtle sensory changes.

It is possible to have one type of processing pattern for one sense, and a different pattern for another. It is also possible to have a combination of patterns, as you will see when completing the following self-assessment. Each of these patterns is discussed in greater detail throughout the book.

POINT TO PONDER...

Are you more tired some days than you are on others? Are there days when you eat less food and days when you overeat? Have you ever had a day when you could not get warm or a day when you were more sensitive to light than you were on other days?

We have all experienced times when our sensory needs fluctuate, so it is important to understand that any sense might be more sensitive one day than another. This also means that our behaviors associated with those senses will fluctuate as well.

Processing Patterns and Relationships

When two people in a relationship process sensory encounters differently, it can cause friction. For example, if one person has an under-sensitive system that craves proprioceptive (deep pressure) input, they may stomp their feet when walking or moving. They may also do things like slam doors because they are subconsciously trying to satisfy their sensory craving. These actions may be too loud for their partner, who has an over-sensitive auditory system. The loud noise from stomping feet and slamming doors irritates them, creating stress.

If one person in a relationship is a tactile craver, they will enjoy holding hands and cuddling with their partner. However, if their partner is an avoider, these touch encounters might overwhelm them. These situations can be misinterpreted by either party, leaving the craver feeling rejected and the avoider feeling annoyed.

Sensory processing does not only affect personal relationships; it impacts social and professional relationships as well. *Therefore, you need this sensory education: it teaches you about your sensory preferences, and it helps you understand how sensory processing shapes people's behavior.*

Sensory Awareness

We have all had moments when we were outside and felt so cold that we had to stop what we were doing to seek a warm place of solace. We also experienced times when a person talked so quietly that we struggled to hear what they were saying. Events such as these are fixed in our memories because we were consciously aware of a sensory imbalance.

Is it possible that we develop habits and routines based on sensory preferences? For example, have you ever wondered why you routinely reach for a favorite coffee mug or why you prefer to sit in a particular chair while watching TV? Or the reason you choose to sit in the middle or end of the row, or in the front or back of the movie theater?

Have you wondered what makes you decide if you should sit alone or by people when entering a meeting room? Was there ever a time when you enjoyed a delicious meal at a restaurant, but when asked by friends to return there in the future, you decline, though you could not readily state the reason why? Or why you choose to

sit in a booth or at a square or round table when dining out? Undoubtedly, your sensory preferences are subconsciously dictating your choices.

Sensory awareness is a conscious understanding of a sensory experience. This includes our sensory likes and dislikes. There is a great deal to learn about the senses and how they shape our lives, including our internal senses, called interoception. Studies have found that inner senses greatly influence our emotional state, decision-making, and behaviors.

To increase your sensory intelligence, you must first learn how to develop your sensory awareness. This begins with an in-depth study of the senses and identifying your processing pattern for each sense. It also includes the ability to recognize how each sense influences your experience in each situation.

Four Steps to Sensory Awareness

Step 1: The first step is to determine your sensory processing pattern for each sense. This will help you start to develop a personalized sensory profile.

Step 2: The second step in developing sensory awareness is learning about each of the sensory systems. Learn how they receive information, their functional roles in our body, and how they can impact our behaviors.

Step 3: The third step is to identify how sensory experiences impact your life. This moment of reflection is of the utmost importance in determining which sensory experiences are calming and which ones arouse your nervous system to energize you.

Step 4: The fourth and final step in this process is to create a personalized sensory action plan to help you manage stress. You can control stress by learning to recognize the sensory events that produce feel-good chemicals in your brain and incorporate them into your life, and by avoiding the ones that increase your stress.

This book will equip you with the tools you need to be successful. It will help you establish a well-balanced, healthy, sensory engagement routine for optimal living.

Life-Changing Moment...

SENSORY OVERLOAD

She is a sweet, creative ten-year-old girl from a loving family, yet most of her days are steeped in frustration, isolation, and anxiety. Bright lights, odors, sounds, and clothing bother her as she is an extremely sensitive child. Rising out of bed each morning begins her exhaustive sensory journey. The change in temperature upon the removal of her much-needed weighted blanket leaves her feeling cold and unprotected.

In the time-sensitive environment before school begins, this young girl tearfully tries on one outfit after another, but the way the clothes fit bothers her. She senses her parents' frustration as they hurry to get ready for work, so she tries to hide her anxiety.

Eventually, she puts on the same dress that she wears to school almost every day. The one that does not hurt her or make her tense. She then heads to the kitchen for breakfast, where the bright lights hurt her eyes, so she bows her head. The smell of fried eggs makes her nauseous. Hungry, but defeated, she retreats to her room.

Later, when her mother drives her to school, she starts to feel sick, but she knows the loud, bumpy, smelly school bus will make her feel even worse, so she tries her best to tolerate the car ride. Upon arriving at school, she begs her mother to take her home. She feels dizzy and nauseous, but no one can see that, so no one understands. Her teacher greets them, assuring her mother that 'she'll be fine' as she ushers the child towards the school's entrance, but the little girl knows she is not okay and feels anxious.

She makes her way to the bright, loud classroom where she must sit on a hard, uncomfortable chair for several hours. Keeping her head down to shield her eyes from the light, she is mocked by a fellow student for 'acting like a baby.' The little girl is lost; she does not know what to say or do. She only knows that she feels sick, and like she does not fit in.

When school is over, she comes to see me for therapy. She is sad, feeling lonely, depressed, and misunderstood. Her mother reports that it was another bad day. Typically, I would offer an analogy to explain to the parent how sensory overload affects their child; however, on this day, her mother had her own story to share.

The mother explained that she had spent the past several hours riding in the car with her boss, who liked to drive fast and braked hard. Her boss also blasted the radio as she touted directives to her passenger between taking puffs of her cigarette. The car was loud and smelled like smoke, making each minute seem like an hour. The mother said that she could not wait to get out of that car and go home. Then she said, "Now I understand what it's like for my daughter being at school every day. The sensory overload is exhausting and upsetting."

DEVELOPING YOUR UNIQUE SENSORY PROFILE

It is now time for you to identify your unique processing pattern for each sense. This fun and engaging activity provides an overview of how sensory encounters impact your behaviors.

 Instructions: Read each of the following scenarios. Determine if the statement describes your behavior *most of the time, some of the time,* or *not at all,* and indicate your answer according to the numerical answer key.

Once you have completed the four sections for each sense, total your answers. You will then record your scores on the sensory profile worksheet and follow the instructions.

THE TACTILE SYSTEM

Detects light touch, firm touch, textures, pain, and temperature

 Please read each of the following statements and answer accordingly:

0   Does not describe you
1   Describes you less than 50% of the time
2   Describes you more than 50% of the time

AVOIDER	INDICATE 0, 1, OR 2
You avoid touching sticky or greasy objects	
You cannot tolerate wearing tight-fitting clothes	
You dislike being barefoot	
You dislike using body lotions	
You dislike being touched or caressed	
You avoid wearing clothes or using blankets because of the way the fabric feels	
TOTAL SCORE	

BYSTANDER	INDICATE 0, 1, OR 2
You stand too close to others	
You are not bothered by the way clothes fit	
You do not mind being touched or caressed	
You do not notice if things are sticky or wet	
You do not notice if food gets on your face when eating	
You are not bothered by holding extremely hot or cold items	
TOTAL SCORE	

CRAVER	INDICATE 0, 1, OR 2
You desire to be touched or caressed	
You prefer being barefoot	
You rub your arms, touch your face, or stroke your hair	
You like to touch almost everything	
You like to touch or fidget items	
You like touching water or things that are wet	
Total Score	

DETECTOR	INDICATE 0, 1, OR 2
You are bothered by tags or seams in clothes	
You wash or rinse your hands more than others	
You brush your teeth more than others	
You limit walking barefoot	
You are particular about the way furniture feels (too hard or too soft)	
You are bothered by the texture of some foods	
TOTAL SCORE	

VESTIBULAR SYSTEM

Detects motion, equilibrium, and spatial orientation

 Please read each of the following statements and answer accordingly:

    0   **Does not describe you**
    1   **Describes you less than 50% of the time**
    2   **Describes you more than 50% of the time**

AVOIDER	INDICATE 0, 1, OR 2
You get dizzy more than others	
You avoid activities like riding a bike or skating	
You dislike most amusement park rides	
You prefer sedentary activities	
You feel unsteady on step stools or ladders	
You have a fear of heights	
Total Score	

BYSTANDER	INDICATE 0, 1, OR 2
You bump into things more than others	
You can spin for long periods and never feel dizzy	
You climb ladders without fear or hesitation	
You drift into a daydream when seated for long periods	
You are not bothered by heights	
You do not experience motion sickness	
Total Score	

CRAVER	INDICATE 0, 1, OR 2
You do not like to sit still for long periods	
You have no fear of heights	
You enjoy fast-moving amusement park rides	
You enjoy driving or riding in a car	
You are a thrill-seeker	
You like to stand and move about over sitting still	
Total Score	

DETECTOR	INDICATE 0, 1, OR 2
You squirm or shift when seated	
You feel unsteady when climbing ladders	
You feel unsteady when riding a bike	
You enjoy slow-moving amusement park rides	
Heights make you nervous	
You prefer a chair that swivels or rocks over a stationary chair	
Total Score	

THE VISUAL SYSTEM

Detects colors, contrast, and movement

 Please read each of the following statements and answer accordingly:

0   **Does not describe you**
1   **Describes you less than 50% of the time**
2   **Describes you more than 50% of the time**

AVOIDER	INDICATE 0, 1, OR 2
You avoid bright lights	
You dislike clutter	
You limit the number of wall hangings on the walls	
You prefer to have the blinds closed	
You prefer solid colors over intricate patterns	
You avoid busy stores or places where there is a lot to see	
Total Score	

BYSTANDER	INDICATE 0, 1, OR 2
You lose your place when reading	
You are not distracted by moving objects	
You do not notice when an item has been moved or is missing	
You are not bothered by bright lights	
You are not bothered by clutter	
You have trouble finding clearly visible items	
Total Score	

CRAVER	INDICATE 0, 1, OR 2
You like to keep the blinds open	
You like bright colors	
You enjoy watching moving objects	
You like knick-knacks	
You like busy environments where there is a lot to see	
You like to doodle	
Total Score	

DETECTOR	INDICATE 0, 1, OR 2
You quickly notice if an item is moved or missing	
Your eyes are slow to adjust from bright to dark	
You prefer having dimmer switches on lights	
You limit the number of knick-knacks or decorations	
You have a limited tolerance to busy environments where there is a lot to see	
You are distracted by clutter	
Total Score	

THE AUDITORY SYSTEM

Detects the pitch, volume, tone, and rhythm of sounds

 Please read each of the following statements and answer accordingly:

0   Does not describe you
1   Describes you less than 50% of the time
2   Describes you more than 50% of the time

AVOIDER	INDICATE 0, 1, OR 2
You tell others to stop making noise	
You prefer silence when reading or working	
You are easily bothered by sounds	
You avoid places that are too loud	
You keep doors and windows closed to reduce the noise	
You need white noise to sleep	
Total Score	

BYSTANDER	INDICATE 0, 1, OR 2
You sleep through your alarm	
You are not bothered by loud sounds	
You are not bothered by noise	
You interrupt others when they are speaking	
You ask others to repeat themselves	
You do not need to hear the TV, music, or white noise to sleep	
Total Score	

CRAVER	INDICATE 0, 1, OR 2
You enjoy loud environments	
You like to have the TV or music on when working	
You sing, hum, whistle, or make sounds throughout the day	
You make noise by tapping your foot or pen	
You need to hear the TV or music to fall asleep	
People ask you to quiet down or lower the volume	
Total Score	

DETECTOR	INDICATE 0, 1, OR 2
Your sleep is easily disturbed by noise	
You frequently adjust the volume of the TV or radio	
You are easily distracted by noise	
You have a limited tolerance to sounds or loud environments	
You quickly notice a new or unusual sound	
You ask others to lower the volume or quiet down	
Total Score	

THE PROPRIOCEPTIVE SYSTEM

Sense of body position, movement, and muscle force production

 Please read each of the following statements and answer accordingly:

0   Does not describe you
1   Describes you less than 50% of the time
2   Describes you more than 50% of the time

AVOIDER	INDICATE 0, 1, OR 2
You refuse to wear tight-fitting clothes	
You do not give or receive hugs	
You will not eat hard, crunchy foods	
You will not wear a heavy winter coat	
You do not like heavy blankets in bed	
You do not enjoy lifting weights or heavy items	
Total Score	

BYSTANDER	INDICATE 0, 1, OR 2
You bump into things more than others	
You spill things more than others	
You stomp your feet when walking	
You slam doors and drawers when closing them	
You drop things more than others	
You are not bothered by blankets that are too heavy or light	
Total Score	

CRAVER	INDICATE 0, 1, OR 2
You enjoy participating in physical activities	
You enjoy giving and receiving hugs	
You bounce your leg when seated	
You bite your fingernails or lips	
You enjoy wrestling or roughhousing	
You need a heavy or weighted blanket to sleep	
Total Score	

DETECTOR	INDICATE 0, 1, OR 2
You are particular about food textures	
You are bothered by someone bumping into you or your chair	
You are particular about the way your clothes feel	
You frequently stretch, bend, or twist	
You have a favorite mug or cup	
You are particular about the weight of your blankets in bed	
Total Score	

THE OLFACTORY SYSTEM
Detects odors and scents

 Please read each of the following statements and answer accordingly:

    0 Does not describe you
    1 Describes you less than 50% of the time
    2 Describes you more than 50% of the time

AVOIDER	INDICATE 0, 1, OR 2
You avoid certain foods because of their odor	
You will only use unscented products	
You avoid people due to odor: body or perfume	
You avoid places due to smell	
Certain odors make you gag or feel nauseous	
You will refuse to wear clothes or use towels due to the way they smell	
Total Score	

BYSTANDER	INDICATE 0, 1, OR 2
Scented products do not bother you	
You do not easily detect foul odors	
You are not bothered by the smell of foods, including fish	
You are not bothered by perfumes	
You do not notice the smell of scented candles or air fresheners	
You do notice if your clothes or shoes smell bad	
Total Score	

CRAVER	INDICATE 0, 1, OR 2
You enjoy smelling scented candles or aromatherapy	
You prefer to wear perfume or cologne	
You like scented products	
You enjoy the smell of a zoo or farm	
You enjoy the smell of food, including fish	
You open doors and windows to enjoy the smell of grass, trees, and flowers	
Total Score	

DETECTOR	INDICATE 0, 1, OR 2
You are quick to notice any smell	
You have a limited tolerance to perfumes	
You notice the smell of a room upon entering	
You have a limited tolerance to scented candles or air fresheners	
You limit your diet due to the smell of food	
You sniff clothes, blankets, or other items before using them	
Total Score	

THE GUSTATORY SYSTEM

Detects tastes and flavors

 Please read each of the following statements and answer accordingly:

     0   **Does not describe you**
     1   **Describes you less than 50% of the time**
     2   **Describes you more than 50% of the time**

AVOIDER	INDICATE 0, 1, OR 2
You are a picky eater who refuses to eat certain foods	
You dislike spicy foods	
You do not like to try new foods	
You prefer bland or familiar foods	
You refuse to eat bitter foods	
You refuse to eat intensely flavored foods like fish	
Total Score	

BYSTANDER	INDICATE 0, 1, OR 2
You do not notice if something tastes bad	
You do not notice if food is spicy	
You do not add salt or spices to food	
You are willing to try new foods	
You are not particular about the taste of food	
You are not bothered by hot sauce on foods	
Total Score	

CRAVER	INDICATE 0, 1, OR 2
You enjoy eating spicy foods	
You like to try new foods	
You add spices or hot sauce to foods	
You like to eat sour or bitter foods	
You like foods with intense flavors	
You like to chew gum or suck on hard candy throughout the day	
Total Score	

DETECTOR	INDICATE 0, 1, OR 2
You have limited tolerance to intense flavors	
You limit your diet, but will occasionally try new foods	
You notice if food has a different or unusual taste	
You have limited tolerance for spices on foods	
You have limited tolerance for sour foods	
You are very particular about the flavor of foods	
Total Score	

SENSORY PROFILE WORKSHEET

Complete the chart below by indicating your total score for sections A-D for each sense. Circle the highest score in each category. This will reveal your overall processing pattern for that sense. It is important to note that sensory processing patterns fluctuate due to medical conditions, stressors, and aging.

This is a subjective assessment; therefore, it is not uncommon for someone to have a combination of processing patterns for each sense. A person who reveals a high score as a detector may also have a similar score in the avoider or craver category. This indicates that as a detector, you tend to crave more or avoid sensory input.

SENSE	A AVOIDER	B BYSTANDER	C CRAVER	D DETECTOR
TACTILE/TOUCH				
VESTIBULAR/BALANCE				
VISUAL/ SIGHT				
AUDITORY/HEARING				
PROPRIOCEPTION/ MOVEMENT				
OLFACTORY/SMELL				
GUSTATORY/TASTE				

THE AMAZING SENSES

OUR AMAZING SENSES

Our senses help us understand the world around us. Each sense is unique and is tasked with a distinct function, yet they work together to create our perception of experiences. The senses help us connect with our environment by receiving information and sending it to our brain for interpretation. How we interpret sensory information will affect our mood, temperament, and behaviors.

In the busyness of life, it is easy to overlook the sensory events that make our lives so special. We experience beautiful sights, melodic sounds, enticing aroma, and comforting touches throughout the day, yet we often fail to savor the fullness that each experience has to offer. Many people enjoy seeing the sun streaming through the trees as they sip their tasty morning coffee. Yet, how often do people cherish things, like the sound of their co-workers laughing in the breakroom or their comfy office chair that swivels and reclines? Unfortunately, we sometimes fail to appreciate a sensory experience until it is gone.

Our senses are quite amazing, and I have found that people become more confident and capable when they learn more about them. The next several chapters are dedicated to teaching you about each of the senses. You will learn how they work, and their role in shaping our perception of an experience. This knowledge is truly life changing. It will not only help you manage stressors; it will help you to live your life to the fullest.

CHAPTER 6

THE TACTILE SYSTEM

Detects light touch, firm touch, textures, pain, and temperature through receptors in the skin

The tactile system is the largest sensory system. It plays a crucial role in our physical, social, and cognitive development by detecting light touch, deep touch, vibration, temperature, and pain. Touch sensations help us determine if a surface is smooth, bumpy, hot, or cold. They also help us identify if an object is sharp, soft, hard, wet, or dry. Our brain interprets these touch encounters to determine if they are safe or dangerous.

The tactile system has two distinct mechanisms: the discriminative system and the protective system. The discriminative system discerns what is touching us and where it is touching our bodies, so we can safely experience our world. We rely on this sense to determine the size, shape, and texture of objects. We also use it to establish social and emotional bonds through pleasurable physical contact.

The protective system has a vastly different responsibility; it determines if a touch encounter is safe or dangerous. This mechanism is quite sensitive, allowing us to feel everything, even the tiniest insect crawling on our skin. It is no wonder that the tactile system is an integral part of our social relationships, academic learning, and protection in this busy world.

A well-developed tactile system is crucial for our success. It enables us to feel things like buttons or zippers, and it helps us locate items that are not visible to our eyes, such as coins in our pocket. When this system functions properly, it allows us to do things like wear clothes comfortably and enjoy walking barefoot in the grass.

The tactile system has a significant impact on our ability to bond emotionally and socially. Tolerance of physical touch is crucial for our social development. This system helps us modulate the touch from a hand, tap on the shoulder, or the possibility of an unwanted contact when standing in lines or crowds.

POINT TO PONDER...

Can tactile processing sensitivities increase our levels of stress and anxiety? When the nervous system interprets a touch experience as a potential threat, it thrusts us into survival mode. This increases the production of adrenaline, norepinephrine, and cortisol, the neurotransmitters that make us feel stress.

How The Tactile System Works

The tactile system contains over seventy percent of the sensory receptors in our body. It receives information from touch receptors located across the outer skin and inside the mouth, ears, and digestive system. It relies on five different nerve receptors to process this incoming information.

The light touch receptors are located close to the surface of the skin and are extremely sensitive. Areas like our lips, genitals, hands, and feet have higher concentrations of these nerve endings. The receptors for pain, temperature, and vibration are also close to the skin's surface, while the receptors that detect touch-pressure are located deep in the dermis.

Touch sensations alert us to what is happening in our environment. They direct our attention to the source of stimulation so we can respond accordingly. If we touch something sharp, we react by pulling away. If a slap on the back is intense, we react by protecting ourselves. How our brain interprets a touch encounter will determine if protective action is required for our survival. Sustained pressure will also activate our defensive mechanism. If the band from our socks or underwear is too tight, the pressure alerts us to possible danger. A repeated warning signal will be sent to the brain to encourage you to remove the garment to ensure that blood circulates properly. These protection principles also work in situations that include extreme temperatures, changes in surface, and pain perception.

Light touch is an integral part of our protective sense: even the smallest crumb left behind on a chair will be detected. Light touch receptors detect if an object is sharp, a surface is textured or if food happens to be smeared on your face. We experience light touch sensations in various ways like grass rubbing against our feet, beads of water trickling down our body, or bed sheets sweeping over our skin. A light touch from a gentle caress or wind stroking our hair might be enjoyable for some people, but it can also elicit pain or anxiety in others. It all depends on how the person's brain processes the sensory event.

Tickling also requires the ability to tolerate light-touch stimulation. It is the rapid stimulation of light-touch receptors that create a tickling sensation. However, this sensation is only pleasant when the pressure and duration are controlled to the person's tolerance. Tickling activates our stress response because it stimulates pain receptors, which is why we pull away. This explains why some people dislike being tickled. Individuals who enjoy tickling other people need to understand that their actions might be causing pain; therefore, they should stop tickling upon request.

> ## POINT TO PONDER...
>
> Why can't we tickle ourselves? The part of the brain called the cerebellum is responsible for controlling our movement. It senses the pattern and force of our touch. Therefore, it anticipates the touch of a self-tickle and notifies the rest of the brain that it is coming. This forewarning mutes the intensity of the sensation.

Deep pressure that comes from a hug or massage tends to be more tolerable than a light touch. Wearing tight-fitting clothes, lifting heavy items, and activities that include pulling, pushing, or jumping also stimulate deep-touch receptors. Most people unknowingly crave deep pressure touch because it increases body awareness, which helps organize their thoughts and reduce stress. The benefit from this type of touch has revolutionized an industry of compression clothing, weighted blankets, and vests. It has also rejuvenated the sales of soft furniture like beanbag or hammock chairs that provide deep pressure.

The tactile system is also responsible for detecting the temperature of an object. It determines if the ground is too hot for bare feet or if the sheets are cold when you get into bed. If a person is under-sensitive and unable to register temperatures properly, it increases their risk of injury from extremely hot or cold items. This has been known to happen with things like ice packs, hot drinks, heating pads, or heated seats in cars. (In some vehicles, heated seats get too hot and have resulted in painful burns. Extreme caution is advised if placing someone with diminished sensation, young children, or advanced-aged adults in heated car seats.)

Vibration is also processed through the tactile system. It stimulates both light touch and deep pressure receptors. It can be very soothing to some or disturbing to others. Many babies sleep best when riding in a car because the vibration helps them to relax. Manufacturers have capitalized on this by developing vibrating chairs, mattress pads, and toys. However, some children cannot tolerate vibration, and their intolerance causes them to cry when riding in a car. Vibration does not only have an effect on children; it can also affect adults. The vibration from cell phones alerts us to a call, while the vibration from riding in a train or car lulls us to sleep. Vibration can be calming or arousing, which explains why vibrating products have become increasingly popular.

The tactile system also processes pain. We

have all witnessed the child who cries while protectively holding his finger from a small cut that happened days earlier. These children are hypersensitive to pain. The residual sensation from that injury registers in their brain as a painful stimulus. Conversely, we have observed people who suffer a sizeable gash in their arm, yet they do not seem to notice any discomfort. Their lack of response may appear to be an admirable trait; but it is a warning that their protective sense is diminished. Hyposensitivity to pain can result in serious harm to the body.

We can all agree that touch is a powerful sense. It is what we long for to feel comforted, protected, and loved. In childhood, parents used touch to wipe the tears from our eyes, kiss our foreheads, and stroke our hair. There is no denying that touch is crucial in our lives.

How Do Touch Encounters Affect Your Life?

Touch is something we seldom think about, but it can have a profound impact on our lives. Consider your morning routine on a chilly morning. You wake up early and push the smooth button to silence the alarm. Then you remove your soft blanket as a surge of cold air sweeps over your body.

Your bare feet feel the soft, plush carpet as you walk to the bathroom. Suddenly, you feel a stabbing sensation from a plastic toy left on the ground. Your feet are then further assaulted by the cold, hard tile of the bathroom floor. The lever of the faucet feels cold to the touch as you turn the water on at the sink. You suddenly feel something sticky on your hands and realize the children left toothpaste smeared on the faucet. Frustrated, you wash your hands with slimy soap and rinse them in the cold water. The soft, plush towel dries your hands until you feel something hard on the fabric. Upon review, you see dried toothpaste left behind by your little ones.

Your tactile system has already experienced something smooth, sharp, warm, cold, soft, hard, sticky, slimy, wet, and dry, and you have only been awake for 5 minutes. Think about how many tactile experiences you will encounter by the end of the day and how each one affects your behaviors.

For example, how do you feel when your toddler hugs you goodbye as you leave for work? You feel the warmth of his body through his soft flannel pajamas as his fluffy hair gently strokes your cheek. The weight of his head rests on your shoulder as he wraps his small arms around your neck. Then his soft lips kiss your cheek to say goodbye. These types of touch experiences are not only pleasurable; they reduce your stress. It truly is amazing how many tactile encounters we experience each day, which is why it is important to recognize how sensory experiences affect our lives.

Signs of Impaired Processing

How can tactile processing impact a person's life? A person may be over-sensitive to one type of touch and under-sensitive to another, and these sensitivities will vary based on age, condition, or circumstance. It is important to remember that our sense of touch is responsible not only for discriminative sensation but also for our protection.

The tactile system has two distinct functions. This explains why some children enjoy roughhousing with friends, yet they scream in horror when their hair is combed or nails are trimmed. Different touch receptors are processing each of these events. The over-sensitive receptors may interpret hair brushing or nail trimming as painful.

The interpretation of touch also applies to clothing. Some people cannot tolerate snug-fitting waistbands or tags in their clothes. These touch encounters are being misinterpreted as a possible threat, causing the person to feel irritated and anxious. Underwear is also a big problem for many people, especially children. It has elasticized bands, thick seams, or waistbands that are bothersome to sensitive systems.

Scratchy material, stiff new clothes, or textured fabrics are also offenders. Messages received from clothing might activate our protective mechanism, which puts us in fight or flight mode. We may choose to ignore the warning signal, hoping our clothes will stretch out or that we adapt to the sensory input. Sometimes our bodies will adapt, but many times they cannot. This sensation then becomes distressing because the misinterpretation is activating our protective mechanism.

Sensations that we perceive as irritating affect our behaviors, mood, and attention span. They increase anxiety and frustration. This is not only

caused by tight-fitting clothing; it can also be caused by loose-fitting clothing. The material from loose-fitting clothes sweeps over the skin, stimulating light-touch receptors. If those receptors are overly sensitive, the touch activates our survival mode. This stress will continue until the 'perceived threat' is removed. Touch sensations from food textures, lotions, soaps, sheets, towels, and furniture can also be misperceived as a possible threat. Inefficient tactile processing sometimes results in a condition called tactile defensiveness.

Tactile Defensiveness

Tactile defensiveness is a pattern of observable behaviors in response to specific touch encounters. People with this condition make every effort to avoid certain experiences. If they are unable to do so, they may over-react to the touch encounter. In adults, tactile defensiveness can trigger a panic attack or make the person anxious. Children may display tantrum type behaviors when they cannot avoid aversive touch experiences. Whether a person is young or old, this condition significantly impacts functional performance, social relationships, and emotional security, contributing to low self-esteem, anxiety, and social isolation.

Impaired Processing in Children

People tend to misunderstand children who have problems with tactile processing. Unlike adults, children do not get to choose their clothing, bedding, or furniture. They also do not have control over their social interactions or opportunities where touch might occur. They are told to hug their aunt or kiss their uncle. Sadly, these directives fail to consider the child's ability to tolerate touch experiences.

A child's refusal can be misconstrued as defiance or disrespect when they are merely responding to their tactile system. This misunderstanding can have more significant consequences than we realize. When a child is scolded for things like not hugging a relative or standing away from the crowd, they feel embarrassed and ashamed. This affects their self-esteem and increases their anxiety.

Children who have an under-sensitive system exhibit very different behaviors. They like to touch everything and have difficulty paying attention because they lack impulse control. These youngsters feel compelled to turn knobs, push buttons, or kick the chair in front of them.

Tactile Processing Patterns

The Avoider

The avoider has an over-sensitive tactile system that makes it difficult for them to tolerate various touch experiences. Some avoiders are unable to wear tight-fitting clothes, while others are bothered by loose-fitting garments. They also cannot handle the feeling of tags, fabrics,

footwear, and even jewelry. Avoiders are also very particular about the texture of furniture, bedding, and towels because they are sensitive to the way each of these feels. Therefore, it is not uncommon for them to have a favorite chair, jacket, or mug.

Their sensitivity will also make it difficult for them to be in crowds, stand in lines, hold hands, and give or receive hugs. Their intolerance to human touch will adversely impact both their personal and professional relationships. In the workplace, the avoider must have the autonomy to control their personal space and choose their supplies to be successful. Their productivity will be affected by sensations that they find offensive. Tactile offenses impact their ability to focus, plan, and organize steps to complete tasks, which affects their temperament and interactions with others.

The Bystander

The bystander has an under-sensitive tactile system. They are not typically bothered by the texture of food, clothes, or touch from others. The bystander may not even notice that they have been touched unless it was an intense touch experience. Their dulled tactile system makes it unlikely that they will detect food on their faces, something sticky on their hands, or misaligned clothes.

Bystanders also lack safety awareness due to their under-sensitive system. This exposes them to a greater risk of injury. They may not remove a garment that is too tight, and they may not be aware that they suffered a cut, or bruise until someone else brings it to their attention. This decreased awareness is especially concerning for the young bystander.

The Craver

The craver has an under-sensitive tactile system that craves more input to process a sensory event. It is not uncommon for a craver to walk barefoot on all kinds of surfaces like grass, sand, or tile. Their craving for tactile experiences often exceeds social norms by prompting them to touch anything that intrigues them. Most touch is pleasing to the craver. They like to pet the dog or touch wet, sticky, dry, or grainy textures. Cravers embrace human touch. They love holding hands or a gentle caress. Sometimes, a craver can appear rude as their desire for touch fails to consider personal space or acceptable boundaries.

The craver's desire for touch can also lead to self-soothing behaviors like twirling their hair, stroking their faces, or tapping their fingers or toes. They also desire oral touch sensation, so they bite on a pen cap, repeatedly lick their lips, or frequently use ChapStick. It is not uncommon for cravers to smoke cigarettes, cigars, or vape as prompted by this sensory craving.

The Detector

Detectors have an over-sensitive tactile system that allows them to detect even the most minute changes. They notice if their favorite shirt feels differently after being washed, and display some of the same behaviors as the avoider, such as limiting their wardrobe because they cannot tolerate certain fabrics.

The detector will notice if a bath towel is new or is a different fabric than the previous one. They are also particular about the feel and fit of their bedding. If the sheets are too big and create wrinkles, or are too tight pulling, up the corners of the mattress, the detector is sure to notice. Detectors also notice the texture and temperature of foods. They limit their diet and are particular about mixing different textures of foods, like yogurt with granola or ice cream with sprinkles.

What Is Touch Hunger?

Touch hunger is a need for emotional and physical touch connection with another person. From a human-needs perspective, the desire to touch and be touched is as important as our need to eat. We crave physical contact. Many people try to satisfy this longing through sexual encounters, but skin hunger is not a sexual lust.

Years ago, a controversial experiment was conducted by psychologist Harry Harlow. In this experiment, infant macaques' monkeys were separated from their mothers at birth. Researchers then gave them two options: a wire surrogate that held a bottle of food, or a cloth-covered proxy that only offered a comforting touch. Each time, the infant monkeys chose the surrogate covered in the soft cloth over the wire one that had the food supply. Harlow's findings were revealing. His study showed that touch-hunger is more powerful than nutritional hunger.

Other studies have substantiated our need for human touch. They found that babies who were deprived of human contact suffered stunted growth and developmental delays. Toddlers who experienced touch neglect in orphanages had difficulty with social bonding, emotional regulation, and executive functions. Current studies that use brain scans discovered physical changes in the brains of individuals deprived of human touch. These findings overwhelmingly support our need for human contact. A lack of human touch has been associated with higher rates of aggression, emotional instability, developmental delays, and cognitive impairments. It has been shown to increase anxiety, depression, mood disorders, and social dysfunction.

The benefits of physical contact include a reduction of anxiety, depression, and illnesses. Physical contact also improves cognitive processing, emotional regulation, and social engagement, and reduces pain.

Today we live in a time where social media is quickly replacing face-to-face encounters. Most professional institutions have a 'no-touch' policy due to fear of ramifications. It is also a time when self-injurious behaviors, anxiety, depression, and substance abuse are spiraling out of control. Touch-hunger research indicates that physical contact is crucial for our development and well-being, so in our current 'no-touch' world, we have to make a conscious effort to fill the void left by social media and 'no-touch' policies. Of course, an individual's ability to process tactile experiences must always be considered.

Calming or Arousing

Ask people what they do to wake themselves up when they feel tired, and many say they splash water on their faces. Most people know that cold water touching the skin is arousing. Many touch experiences like a cold drink or a cool breeze will also stimulate our nervous system. However, many people fail to recognize that removing our clothes for a shower, rubbing a textured loofah sponge over our body, and drying off with a towel also excite the nervous system.

There are also a multitude of touch experiences that make us feel calm and relaxed. For instance, warm water, hot air blowing from a hairdryer, and the gentle tug on our hair when brushing can make us feel calm and composed. A morning hug, slipping our feet into plush slippers, and rubbing our fingers over a furry pet can also be quite relaxing. People talk about unwinding in a warm bath, easing into a soft sweatshirt, and then sinking into their favorite chair to relax. For some, pushing their bare feet into the hot sand, feeling waves caress their body, and the sun's warmth against their skin makes a day at the beach relaxing. These types of experiences soothe our nervous system.

Food textures can also be calming or alerting. Dry, crunchy foods tend to be more alerting, while soft, chewy, or mushy type foods tend to be more calming. An ice-cold drink will arouse your system while the warmth from a hot liquid creates a sense of calm. It is important to recognize how sensory experiences affect you so you can readily discern which encounters will energize you or calm you down.

POINT TO PONDER...

Some sensory inputs calm a nervous system that is overwhelmed, while others provide stimulation to arouse a fatigued system. This insight will help you understand how sensory experiences can improve your attention and energy while reducing anxiety and stress.

CHAPTER 7

THE VESTIBULAR SYSTEM

*Detects motion, equilibrium & spatial
orientation through receptors in the inner ear*

The vestibular system is important because it provides support to our other senses. Since nearly everything we do involves some degree of movement, the vestibular system plays a vital role in our lives. This system is responsible for our balance and spatial orientation. It detects linear (forward and back) and rotational (round and round) motion. It also plays a crucial role in developing our muscle tone and stabilizing our visual field.

A healthy vestibular system enables us to feel confident and secure because we know our body will be able to adapt to postural changes with certainty. This confidence allows us to attend to tasks, organize our thoughts, and sequence our movements. It is no wonder the vestibular system serves as the foundation of our other senses.

POINT TO PONDER...

Insufficient vestibular processing has been linked to increased stress and low self-esteem. Impairments can cause a multitude of symptoms, including vertigo, visual disturbances, and problems with balance. This affects a person's sense of security, emotional stability, memory, and self-perception.

How The Vestibular System Works

The inner ear, located deep within the ear, consists of the cochlea and the vestibular system.

The cochlea is responsible for our ability to hear and will be discussed in later chapters. The vestibular system detects movement and the position of our head so we can maintain our balance.

The vestibular system is made up of two sacs and three semi-circular canals. The sacs contain millions of crystals that detect upward, downward, forward, and backward movements while the canals each detect a specific motion. The horizontal canal tells us if our head is turning right or left. The superior canal determines if our head is leaning toward our shoulder, and the posterior canal detects when our head is nodding up and down. When we move our head, the fluid in the canals shifts over tiny hairs, sending information to the brain about our position.

This complex system detects if our body is bending forward, leaning back, standing, sitting, or lying down. It provides us with information about the direction and speed of our motion. It determines if we are walking up or down a hill and if our acceleration is increasing or decreasing. It also works with visual and proprioceptive systems to manage our balance, movement, and visual skills and is responsible for our Vestibular-Ocular Reflex (VOR). This reflex stabilizes images on our retina, so they do not become blurry as we move our heads.

Signs of Impaired Processing

An under or over-sensitive system can each have a significant impact on our ability to succeed in tasks. An under-sensitive vestibular system needs intense input to stimulate the nervous system. It can cause people to have trouble concentrating or drift into a daydream when seated.

Some people crave vestibular stimulation and will stimulate their system by playing sports or doing things like riding a bike or running. They may even engage in high-risk activities such as cliff diving or bungee jumping to get the amount of input their bodies need. They prefer chairs that swivel, rock, or recline to arouse their system when seated and will frequently stand to stretch after sitting for an extended period.

People who have an over-sensitive vestibular system exhibit very different behavior. They experience motion sickness, get dizzy easily, and feel nervous when moving. Their disequilibrium makes them anxious because they feel like they are falling. Their inability to modulate changes in gravity can result in Gravitational Insecurity (GI).

Gravitational Insecurity

Gravitational insecurity (GI) is a condition that causes people to experience excessive fear when they are unable to maintain an upright posture or when their feet are not planted firmly on the ground. GI causes an individual to panic because they feel like they are falling. This affects their ability to walk on changing surfaces like sidewalks or sand. It also impacts their ability to lean their head forward or back.

We have all experienced a similar sense of dread when we unexpectedly slipped on ice or wet leaves. It is jarring to lose control of our footing and balance. We can only imagine how difficult it must be for people with gravitational insecurity to manage everyday movements. Activities, like running, climbing ladders, or leaning back in a chair, will cause a significant amount of stress. Gravitational insecurity can also contribute to a fear of heights, elevators or escalators, and reclining chairs like those found in the dentist's office or hair salon. In children, it can make them feel insecure and fearful when going on sliding boards, climbing on monkey bars, or playing on playground equipment.

Impaired Processing in Children

Children who have an under-sensitive vestibular system will lean their heads on their hands when seated or prop themselves up against something when standing. They continually sway or shift their weight to move their body. This prompts repeated directives by adults to sit still. Their inability to modulate vestibular input makes them clumsy and inattentive. It will also affect their motor-planning skills. Sitting for extended periods may be extremely difficult for these children. They seem antsy because they need to move to satisfy their vestibular needs.

Impaired processing will also impact their ability to participate in everyday activities such as dining out or sitting for a car ride. These children may run instead of walk and are known for being rambunctious. These youngsters would benefit significantly from periodic movement breaks throughout the day to keep them alert and engaged. Children who have an over-sensitive vestibular system may refuse to participate in certain activities. When asked to do seemingly simple tasks, they may suffer a meltdown, fearing insecurity from moving or bending. They might also suffer from a poor self-image if they have been labeled 'difficult or bad' by frustrated adults.

POINT TO PONDER...

People are only able to relate to what they personally experience when encountering a particular sensory input. For example, if someone always feels unsteady when moving, they have no way of knowing what it is like to feel sure-footed. If a person dislikes touching certain textures, they cannot understand why others find them appealing.

It's important to understand that each person has their own unique ability to process sensory information. A lack of education about sensory processing contributes to anxiety and depression. It can prompt people to ask themselves 'what is wrong with me' when they are unable to perform like their peers.

Vestibular Processing Patterns

The Avoider

Avoiders are over-sensitive to vestibular stimulation, causing them to avoid movement-related activities. They want to engage like other people but cannot because they feel unsteady, nauseous, disoriented, or dizzy. Their over-sensitive system exposes them to the risk of injury because they cannot modulate positional changes. They may avoid activities like riding a bike, flying, sailing, or riding in a car. Avoiders are likely to prefer sedentary activities for recreation, limiting activities that require positional changes or quick movements.

The Bystander

The bystander has an under-sensitive system, which makes their vestibular processing sluggish. This affects their ability to navigate around furniture, objects, or people. It affects their motor planning skills, causing them to stumble or trip when moving. Bystanders do not specifically seek out vestibular input, nor do they avoid it. It may take them longer than their peers to engage in movement-related activities because they cannot coordinate their movements. This under-reaction can make them appear to be lazy if they sit around until prompted to move. They also drift into a daydream when seated because they need stimulation to remain alert.

The Craver

The craver is the person who seeks vestibular input because they need intense stimulation to feel organized, balanced, and in control. Cravers are in constant motion. They shift while seated or standing, and have difficulty keeping still during lectures. These movements help stimulate their vestibular system. They are regularly active people who find it hard to sit still for extended periods. They enjoy activities that include spinning, rocking, jumping, dancing, walking, or running.

The craver enjoys long car rides, flying in planes, train rides, or boating. They like to do things like biking, surfing, sailing, skiing, or skating, and they love to drive any motorized vehicle. Quenching this vestibular craving helps keep them alert and focused so that they can concentrate on other things.

The Detector

The detector has an over-sensitive system that over-reacts to vestibular input. They may not avoid movement-related activities but are reluctant to engage in active sports, and they only participate for as long as they can tolerate the activity. Detector's may hold the railing when using the stairs, drag their hands along the walls as they walk, and they might appear nervous. Their over-sensitivity may cause motion sickness or make activities like running, jumping, or dancing difficult.

Calming or Arousing

Vestibular stimulation can have a profound effect on the nervous system. Bouncing, jumping, spinning, running, or dancing can be exhilarating and make you feel alert while rocking or swaying motions tend to be soothing and calming. Fifteen minutes of vestibular input can produce several hours of benefit. For instance, if you are seated for an extended time and start to feel drowsy, standing up and walking around will energize you, giving you the energy to work several more hours. Climbing stairs, spinning in a swivel chair, or doing simple exercises can also increase your energy and focus by stimulating your vestibular receptors.

Rotational movement, like spinning, is the most powerful form of vestibular input. This explains why amusement park rides that spin or turn upside down are so popular. Rotational movements that last too long or movement that abruptly starts and stops can result in a vestibular overload. Signs of a vestibular overload include dizziness, nausea, sweating, flushing, anxiety, and emotional instability. These symptoms can linger for an extended time following the input. Activities like rocking, riding in a car, or running can calm the nervous system. Slow, repetitive movement can be used to help people relax and reduce anxiety. This explains why people find solace relaxing in a hammock, riding on a boat, or floating in the pool.

POINT TO PONDER...

In schools, teachers like to create cluster seating by arranging the desks to form a large rectangle. Children seated along the side must turn their heads to see the board. They must turn back to look down and refocus their eyes on their work. This repeats throughout the day, causing a sensory overload. This makes the child feel fatigued and disorganized. It also affects their ability to learn. I encourage parents to advocate for forward-facing seating in all classrooms.

Teachers may not realize how this seating arrangement impacts their students' behavior and academic performance. It would not be much different from watching a movie in a theater where the chairs faced the room's side instead of the front of the theater. It would be uncomfortable, distracting, and exhausting.

CHAPTER 8

THE VISUAL SYSTEM

Detects Colors, Contrast, and Movement through receptors in the eyes

People depend on their vision to explore this colorful, extraordinary world. More than two-thirds of the information we receive comes in through our eyes. We learn by observation, tending to trust what we see. We use this information to determine if we like something, as we are often swayed by the way things look. We also rely on this important sense to guide our movements and to keep us safe.

The visual system plays a crucial role in our social development. Ninety percent of communication is nonverbal, with more than half of that interpreted from facial expressions and body gestures. We observe people's gestures with our eyes, relying on these social cues to respond appropriately. Our vision also helps keep us safe. It spots dangerous situations, an obstacle in our path, or a suspicious character lurking nearby. It helps us do things like find the key that will open the front door or inspect a room upon entering. Our vision provides us with a wealth of information, more than could ever be discussed in one book. For that reason alone, we value our sight.

The visual system works together with our vestibular and proprioceptive systems to facilitate movement and balance. It also supports the tactile system by allowing us to see what our touch receptors are feeling. Undeniably, our sense of sight plays a crucial role in everything we do, yet most people know little about how visual information is processed.

How The Visual System Works

The visual system works by detecting contrast, colors, and movement through light receptors

93

located in our eyes. This allows us to visualize shapes, forms, and depths. Visual images are created when light passes through the pupil and get absorbed on cells located in the retina. The cells then transmit electrochemical impulses to either the cones or the rods. Cones are located in the center of the pupil, detecting colors and high acuity. The rods are located in the periphery of the pupil and are responsible for our vision in dim lighting. The electrical impulses pass from neuron to neuron until they reach the optic nerve. The optic nerve then sends the information to the brain for interpretation.

How the brain organizes and interprets this information is called visual processing. Visual processing is the ability to make sense of what is seen through the eyes. It enables our eyes to do things like follow moving objects, shift our gaze from near to far, and find an item in a busy environment. It plays a vital role in our ability to learn, and it enables us to see how near or how far away we are from other people or objects. Undeniably, visual processing has a significant impact on our daily function.

Visual Processing Skills

Depth Perception: The ability to see things in three dimensions: length, width, and depth, to perceive how far away or how near a person or object is to where you are located.

Visual Discrimination: The ability to identify similarities and detect subtle differences to differentiate one object from another. Examples would include seeing the difference between similar-looking letters, matching items, and noticing small details.

Visual-Motor Integration: The ability to coordinate hand or foot movements using feedback from the eyes. Examples include handwriting, texting, or navigating around obstacles.

Visual Tracking: The ability to maintain focus and smooth eye movements as your eyes follow a moving object. Examples include moving the eyes left to right to read without losing your place or following a Frisbee that was thrown to you.

Form Constancy: The ability to recognize a shape, symbol, or form when the size, position, or design changes. Examples include identifying street signs, various utensils (a large spoon and small spoon) and a letter when written in different fonts: A, *A*, *A*

Figure-Ground Perception: The ability to identify one specific piece of information from a busy background. Examples include maintaining your place when reading, locating a specific item on the grocery store shelf, or finding a particular sock in the drawer. Perhaps you may recall the Where's Waldo books. The ability to spot Waldo requires figure-ground skills.

Visual Closure: The ability to correctly recognize an object, number, or word when it is not entirely visible. Examples include identifying a word or phrase that is only partially revealed, recognizing a logo, or a street sign when it is partially occluded.

Visual Memory: The ability to recall visual details of what you have seen. Examples include copying information from a sign or board or recalling information for a test or form.

Visual Sequence Memory: The ability to remember the visual details in the correct sequence. Examples include reading directions or an instruction sheet.

Visual-Spatial Relationships: The ability to identify one's position in space. Examples include how close you stand to others, how you space your letters when writing, and how accurately you judge distances when pouring a drink into a cup.

Visual Processing Speed: The ability to make sense of incoming visual information quickly. This could impact any timed activity, your response time, and maintaining the pace of action. Examples include starting to drive when the traffic light turns green or stopping when it turns red. It also includes your ability to detect an oncoming object so you can safely move out of harm's way.

The following eye movements also contribute to our sensory experience:

Fixation: The ability to focus and maintain a steady gaze.

Saccades: The ability to shift our fixation quickly, or focused gaze, from one object to another, like when we look at a street sign and then the car speedometer.

Pursuits: This allows the eyes to move smoothly to follow moving objects like when we are driving. The head remains stationary as the eyes smoothly move and follow the visual target.

These are the visual processing skills that are necessary for us to achieve success in performing daily tasks. If things like handwriting, playing ball, or locating items in a store are difficult for you, it may be due to a visual processing disorder.

Visual Processing

The clarity of an image alone does not determine our perception of what is seen; our perception also relies on our ability to process visual information. Most people know little about visual processing. They are familiar with the standard eye exam that tests acuity, the sharpness of an image; however, 20/20 vision does not mean a person is processing visual information correctly.

Visual processing is how the brain *interprets* information received through the eyes. There is so much to learn about visual processing that several books are exclusively devoted to this topic. My goal is to familiarize you with the many aspects of visual processing so you can understand how your processing ability impacts your life.

A visual processing disorder (VPD) means that a person is not processing visual information correctly. This can affect them in a variety of different ways. If their depth perception is impaired, they could misperceive the distance between them and an on-coming vehicle, putting them in harm's way. Impaired depth perception can also impact their ability to do things like pour a drink, catch a ball, or walk down the stairs. An informal way to evaluate your depth perception is to complete the following exercise.

Place the circle at eye level, approximately 18 inches away from your face. Point your index finger up to the sky, aligning your finger's base to the tip of your nose. Move your finger forward approximately 6 inches away from your face and focus your vision on the grey circle. You should see two 'transparent' fingers. Next, focus your gaze on your finger; you should see two distinct circles. (Figures 1 and 2).

FIGURE 1   FIGURE 2

How did you do? If you saw two fingers and two distinct circles, both of your eyes are working together. If you did not see two circles or two fingers, one eye might be stronger than the other. If so, the next exercise will help you determine eye dominance.

Position your finger as previously instructed. Focus on the circle and close your right eye. Your finger should appear to the right side of the circle (Figure 3). Now repeat with your left eye. Your finger should appear to the left side of the circle (Figure 4).

FIGURE 3   **FIGURE 4**

How did you do? If your finger appeared to the side of the circle when each eye was tested, you should have functional binocular vision. If your finger appeared over the circle when either eye was closed, then one eye is more dominant than the other. This could affect your depth perception. If you suspect there is a problem, you should consult with a developmental optometrist who can provide you with professional care.

 Here is another exercise that can help you understand the importance of visual processing. Below there are two parallel lines. Which line is longer?

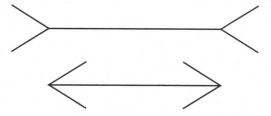

If you said the top line, you are incorrect. Both lines are the same length. Feel free to measure them. The top line appears longer because the endpoints are extending away from the midpoint, creating an optical illusion.

Although these exercises are intriguing, they were included to demonstrate how visual processing affects what is seen through the eyes.

Signs of Impaired Visual Processing

A person can have 20/20 vision but still have impaired visual processing skills. Processing impairments affect each person differently. It can cause people to be clumsy by spilling drinks or careless when they are unable to locate an item that is obvious to everyone else. Some impairments cause people to be distracted by moving objects, like the blinking cursor on their computer screen. These processing impairments can adversely impact a person's accuracy, productivity, and in some instances, their safety.

An impairment makes it difficult for a child to complete school assignments accurately. It would also explain why some adults overlook important details in documents or applications. Impairments can even impact an individual's visual-motor skills. Visual-motor skills are necessary to do things like write a letter or manipulate fasteners on clothes. Sadly, these impairments often go undiagnosed, leaving a person wondering why reading, playing sports, or performing daily tasks is hard for them.

When a person craves visual stimulation, they seek out activities like action-packed video games, events with large crowds, and they prefer bright or intricate designs over solid colors. They enjoy things that stimulate their visual system, which is why cravers like to open the blinds, sit by the window when traveling, and leave the TV on throughout the day.

People who are over-sensitive to visual stimuli will avoid stimulation. They reduce clutter and keep things neat and organized to minimize visual details. They prefer to keep closet doors closed, window shades down, and lights dimmed. Too many faces or objects to look at might result in fatigue or anxiety. Visual overload will also have an effect on a person's mood, productivity, and behavior.

Impaired Processing in Children

Children with impaired processing will have the same challenges as adults; however, children lack the autonomy to regulate how long they are exposed to visual stimuli. These children may be subjected to over-stimulation, which affects their demeanor and behavior.

In school, children must read books, look at the board, and complete written assignments under bright fluorescent lights. This can be difficult for a child with a visual impairment. They get anxious and overwhelmed when doing things in a classroom full of distractions. Impairments make simple tasks hard, such as writing neatly between the lines or aligning numbers for math equations. They can also impact a person's ability to read or locate a specific place on a page and affect their ability to focus and attend.

Visual disturbances also impact recreational activities like playing video games, riding a bike, or playing ball games. Incompetence in these areas will not only embarrass the child; it makes them the target of jokes. This social humiliation, along with their under-achievement in school, creates anxiety and low self-esteem. You can now understand how sensory processing impairments cause of many of life's problems.

Life-Changing Moment...

WHY BORDERS ARE IMPORTANT

Have you ever wondered why pages in a book have borders on all sides? These blank spaces allow our eyes to know where to start and end. Imagine how difficult it would be to read a letter or book if the words began at the top of the page, stopped at the bottom, and went from one side to the other without spaces for borders. The reader would feel overwhelmed by this bombardment of information. Borders provide a much-needed break that allows us to organize and comprehend information.

Children who have difficulty with visual processing benefit from modified worksheets that reduce the number of paragraphs, math problems, or details on the page. This increases blank space. Adults can also benefit from these types of modifications, and from using bullet points or numerical lists.

These days, our lives tend to mimic the page that has no borders: news stories, educational information, entertainment, and social connections are available continuously on our many devices. This bombardment of information is overwhelming and makes life stressful and fatiguing. It is important to recognize that much like the borders on a page, our lives also need boundaries, defining where the busyness starts and where it should end. We need to set limits to make life less stressful and more enjoyable.

Visual Processing Patterns

The Avoider

The avoider has an over-sensitive visual system. This causes them to avoid places that have a lot of people, flashing lights, or things to see. Therefore, they dislike places like stores or malls because too much visual information can make them feel nauseous, exhausted, or anxious. Visual overload can affect their mental health and physical well-being. This is also the reason they need to keep things organized so they can reduce visual clutter.

Avoiders get anxious in messy environments, but they often do not realize that visual stimulation is the culprit. They also tend to be over-sensitive to light or glare. This is the reason they close blinds during the day, turn lamps off in the evening, or dim their computer screens. They might even wear sunglasses or a hat on a cloudy day to help to block visual stimulation.

The Bystander

The bystander has an under-sensitive visual system. This makes it hard for them to detect visual information. They overlook important details when reading a contract, letter, or book. They might also fail to notice their exit when traveling or see an obstacle in their path because of their sluggish system. Bystanders have trouble locating items in the store, and when the store clerk finds it, they wonder how they missed it themselves. These seemingly small events can be a source of stress for the bystander.

It can also cause stress when the bystander must be reminded to do things like closing the closet door or turning the flame off on the stove. The bystander insists that they did not notice these things, nor did they see the coffee they spilled on the floor. These situations will not only cause stress for the bystander, but they also create stress for others.

The Craver

The craver is the person who wakes up and immediately turns on the lights and the TV. They open the blinds, pausing for a moment to look outside. While eating breakfast, the craver continually looks at their phone, watch, or laptop, and every so often, they glance at the television for a moment. They do all these things to stimulate their under-sensitive visual system.

Cravers are also distracted easily by visual activity. Colors, patterns, or moving objects will catch their attention and interrupt their work or social interaction. Their need for visual stimulation explains why they like to have knick-knacks or wall hangings in their home or office. They need an assortment of various designs, colors, shapes, and sizes to satisfy their subconscious longing for visual stimulation.

The Detector

The detector has an over-sensitive system that causes them to notice even the slightest visual details. They quickly identify changes in the environment that most people overlook. For example, they will notice if the end table was moved closer to the couch or if the lamp's light bulb was changed to a soft white bulb from a bright white one. They see every crumb on the counter, every smear on the glass, and even the few dust particles streaming in the sunlight. Detectors can be extremely efficient at tasks because of their ability to detect visual information, but this same visual efficiency can also cause distractibility.

POINT TO PONDER...

Every person does not process sensory experiences in the same way. For example, many people find bright, colorful, flashing lights to be arousing and stimulating, while others may find these sights to be calming. We must remember that sensory experiences affect people differently and that the frequency, duration, and intensity of the sensory input also help form our perception of a sensory experience. It is also important to recognize that we may be more sensitive to input one day than another.

Calming or Arousing

What does a flashing light do? It catches our attention. This is the reason emergency vehicles use flashing lights. Things that move arouse our nervous system because they trigger our protective mechanism. The ability to detect movement has the potential to save our lives. Fast-moving objects, like a ball soaring through the air or a wasp buzzing around our face, arouse our system as well.

Bright colors, busy designs, and engaging visual environments are also known to be stimulating. Light excites us each morning. Bright lights used in schools and offices keep us alert, while dim lights produce a sense of calm. Light is essential, which is why light therapy is popular in many parts of the world. Exposure to a specific intensity of light each day has been found to reduce signs of depression. Cascading and repetitious images, like fish swimming in a fish tank or tall grass blowing in the wind, can relax us by lulling the nervous system. Earth-tone colors are also tranquil; and cascading, repetitious movements like ocean waves, tend to relax us.

The Science Behind Colors

Colors and lines significantly impact the way we feel. Research has found that colors and lines influence our mood, spending habits, and perception of people or places. Today, there is a wealth of information about color science and how these visual inputs shape our lives.

Studies found that the color red incites passion and causes us to react. Black conveys power, but it can also have a calming effect. Greens and blues are natural tones that make us feel safe. We tend to trust these colors, which is why many banks use them in their logo. Yellow is the first color the eye detects. It will catch our attention when combined with another color. Earth tones tend to be calming, while vibrant colors stimulate our nervous system.

Did you know that lines can affect your nervous system as well? A horizontal line produces a calming effect because it is consistent with the horizon. Circular and flowing lines are soothing, helping us to feel relaxed. Diagonal and zig-zag lines indicate movement, which energizes the nervous system, and vertical lines arouse the nervous system, making us feel safe.

Many things create lines. We see lines in structures, fashion, blinds, and advertisements. Most people do not recognize the role they have on our mood and stress levels. Unique colors also make an impact by stimulating the nervous system because they are unfamiliar. Images that include a human face rouse our nervous system because we detect human faces before any other visual input.

These are just some examples of how visual inputs can affect us. There are far too many to list, but this demonstrates how sensory experiences impact our mood, perceptions, and temperament. This knowledge will help you create a stress-free environment that will allow you to enjoy the happy, fulfilling life you deserve.

POINT TO PONDER...

Do you recall instructions or directions better if you look at them or if you hear them? How information is presented will affect your ability to process and remember it. We all have one sense that is more dominant than another. Some people are visual learners, while others rely on hearing. Others may experience the world through their sense of touch. Although our senses work together, we will often rely on one sense more than another.

CHAPTER 9

THE AUDITORY SYSTEM

Detects Pitch, Volume, Tone, and Rhythm of Sounds through the Ear

The auditory system energizes, educates, informs, and soothes us, but most importantly, it protects us. This system allows us to enjoy sounds like music, laughter, and conversations. It detects verbal exchanges, such as instructions and informational announcements. It is busy hearing sounds throughout the day and night to keep us informed and safe.

Our ability to adequately receive and process information we hear can have a profound effect on our behaviors. For instance, many people find the rhythmic sound of rain or the hum from a fan relaxes them, while a loud noise from a cheering crowd energizes them. These are examples of how auditory inputs contribute to our well-being. Sounds permeate our world, and some of these noises can be bothersome.

The sounds that contribute to stress may not be obvious; sometimes, they are subtle or repetitious noises. We are continuously exposed to distressing sounds throughout the day: babies crying, alarms, or sirens will activate our stress response, but less obvious noise also increases cortisol production. Notification sounds from cell phones prompt us to react by stimulating the production of cortisol. Researchers have found that the level of cortisol continues to increase until we look at our phones. Repeated exposure to distressing sounds, whether from our own device or one nearby, contributes to our stress.

Environmental sounds will also trigger cortisol production like the noise that indicates the dishwasher completed its cycle or the bell that announces the elevator has arrived at your floor.

Most of us appreciate the sounds' function but failed to recognize their role in increasing anxiety. A loud, startling sound thrusts us into fight or flight mode, affecting our breathing and heart rate. This type of noise occurs throughout the day, from slamming doors to objects dropped on the ground.

The loud noise from an alarm clock will also activate our protective mechanism. This disturbing sound wakes us by stimulating cortisol production, creating stress before we even get out of bed. You can easily eliminate this stressor by using an alarm clock that utilizes a soft tone, a wake-up light system, or a vibrating disk system to wake you. Alarm clocks that gradually increase the volume of sounds will also help to reduce stress.

Our ability to hear is crucial to our survival because sounds alert us to possible danger. The beeping noise from a smoke detector or the sound of glass breaking at night helps keep us safe. Distinct sounds, like the sound of water dripping or food burning, will also activate our protective mechanism.

The many sounds in this world can be overwhelming because we detect noise throughout the day and night. Unlike eyes that have eyelids to limit input, ears are not designed to prevent noise reception. The downside of having this around the clock system is that it cannot stop detecting sounds, including those that add to our stress and affect our well-being.

Noise-related studies have found that noise impacts our lives in the following ways:

- Elevated noise levels have been linked to a 200% increased risk of anxiety and depression in adults, and emotional distress in children.

- Indicators of depression and anxiety increased by annoyance from noise.

- Noise pollution can trigger the body's stress response, which increases stress hormone levels.

- Noise pollution has been shown to increase health problems, such as heart disease, high blood pressure, and stroke. It is also linked to impaired cognitive functions.

- Loud noises have been found to slow the healing process. Studies found that hospital patients exposed to loud noise from visitors, staff, TV's, hospital equipment, and alarms healed more slowly than patients who were in a quiet environment.

- A typical conversation is approximately 50dB (Decibels). Prolong noise over 110dB can cause irreversible hearing loss. (If you would like to monitor the sounds in your environment, you can download the free decibel meter app on your phone or tablet.)

- Any sound over 85dB can cause hearing loss after eight hours of continuous exposure. When the volume increased to 100dB, the hearing loss occurred after only 15 minutes.

- When a fully inflated balloon pops, the sound registers at 168dB, which is 4dB's higher than the sound of a 12-gauge shotgun; this sudden, loud noise activates cortisol production, which increases our stress.

- Offices that have an open floor plan recorded a decrease in worker productivity by more than two-thirds. The various noises in the environment affect the employees' ability to recall data and perform tasks while increasing epinephrine levels; however, more than half of today's offices are currently using an open floor plan design.

These studies have also found that sounds have a positive impact on our health. They discovered that natural sounds are the most effective in reducing stress. This includes ocean sounds, water rushing down a stream, leaves rustling in the wind, and birds chirping. Today, white noise machines have become quite popular. Many include manufactured sounds of nature; however, these sounds were not as effective in reducing stress as natural sounds. Studies have also found that listening to classical music or binaural beats (different sound frequencies played in each ear) improves attention, productivity, and recall of information, while also reducing anxiety.

POINT TO PONDER...

Studies found that instrumental music played continuously at 70dB in professional environments improved efficiency, creativity, and overall satisfaction in the workplace. It also improved employee retention.

How Music Affects Stress

We should always consider the influence that music has on our lives when discussing sounds because tones, rhythm, and lyrics can significantly impact our emotional state. Researchers discovered that specific songs reduce anxiety by as much as 10%. They also studied the effect of upbeat music and how it stimulates a cortical charge in the brain that energizes the nervous system. This increases attention, problem-solving, and critical thinking skills. People also exercised for extended periods when listening to upbeat music.

Music has the potential to evoke a wide range of emotions. Patriotic songs make us feel proud, love songs spark romance, nostalgic songs help us reminisce, and hymns ignite spirituality. Upbeat music excites us, and sad songs make us melancholy, but other songs can also have an effect on us. The powerful impact that music has on us cannot be overstated, so it is important to recognize how music impacts our lives.

Noises meant to produce stress, like those heard in horror movies, build tension to thicken the plot. Sometimes these dark tones are used in popular music, making the listener feel hopeless or full of rage. Lyrics can also affect us by promoting hate and violence. For this reason, it is important to recognize how sounds are impacting our lives. Although most sounds enhance our lives, some are adding to our stress.

How The Auditory System Works

The auditory system is a sophisticated, yet delicate system divided into three parts: the outer ear, the middle ear, and the inner ear. The outer ear collects sound waves. The sound waves vibrate the eardrum that separates the outer and middle ear. The vibration continues into the inner ear, causing the fluid in the cochlea (small snail-like structure) to vibrate. The fluid stimulates hair cells, creating an electrical impulse that travels along the auditory nerve to the brain that interprets the sound.

This system works by detecting the pitch, volume, tone, and rhythm of sounds. The time and context in which we hear a sound determines if the noise reduces our stress or increases it. For example, footsteps approaching your house in the afternoon may indicate your children are home from school, but footsteps outside your home in the middle of the night alert you to danger, activating your survival system and increasing your stress.

Sounds can affect us in many ways. The sound of dry leaves crunching under our feet when we walk, the gentle hush of a summer breeze, or the uplifting music of children laughing are noises that make us feel happy. The sound of someone chewing their food, tapping their fingernails, or moving about on a squeaky chair can make us feel anxious. These types of irritating sounds can significantly contribute to our stress. We can all agree it is hard to avoid noise. Although we may not be actively listening, we continually hear noises in our environment that are affecting our lives.

Hearing sounds is not the same as processing them. Hearing means we detect noise, while auditory processing refers to the ability to make sense of what is heard through our ears. The ability to listen to sounds and turn them into useful information requires the following auditory processing skills:

Figure-Ground Discrimination: This is the ability to differentiate relevant sounds from background noise. The computer monitor's buzzing sound or the TV playing in the background are examples of noises we must try to filter out. Figure-ground allow us to attend to sounds that we deem relevant.

Auditory Discrimination: This is the ability to distinguish between different sounds like hearing "I'm looking for my hat" when the statement was actually "I'm looking for my cat." It also helps us detect an unusual sound when starting the car or recognizing when someone is calling our name.

Auditory Closure: The ability to understand auditory information when some of the auditory information is missing. For example, when you reach for a pot on the stovetop and someone yells, "Be careful, it's...." Auditory closure helps us to complete the sentence with the word 'hot.'

Auditory Memory: This is the ability to recall what we hear. We use it to remember instructions for an assignment or a person's name when first introduced.

Auditory Sequencing: This is the ability to understand and recall the order of what you heard. For example, when someone gives you directions and tells you to turn right, go two blocks and then turn left, you need to recall those directions in that exact order to get to your destination.

Auditory Spatial Relations: This is the ability to localize sounds. It helps us determine where a sound is coming from and whether it is near or far away. It also helps determine if the distance between us and the sound is increasing or decreasing.

Auditory Tracking: This is the ability to follow sounds. It helps us hear a car's sound as it travels closer to our home or drives farther away.

Auditory Processing Speed: This refers to how quickly we can respond to a sound. For example, how fast we react when hearing 'ready, set, go,' or responding when someone calls our name.

Auditory Attention: This refers to our ability to focus on verbal communication or noises. For example, it helps to remain attentive to someone speaking.

Auditory Comprehension: This refers to our ability to understand verbal communication.

The difference between our ability to hear sounds or process them is often confusing; however, this tutorial will explain why someone can pass a hearing test yet still have problems processing auditory information.

Listening is a complex process that relies on efficient processing skills. These skills enable us to filter out irrelevant noise, and they help us to distinguish words being spoken. If a person has impaired processing, they might hear sounds but have difficulty discerning the information because most of the sounds we hear are detected through air conduction.

Air Conduction and Bone Conduction

Air conduction is when sound waves travel through the air and stimulate receptors by vibrating the eardrum. The quality of these sounds is impacted by the distance between the source and the listening ear. Extraneous noise will also affect the quality of the sound. *Bone conduction* occurs when sounds vibrate the skull bone. The vibration stimulates the inner ear, bypassing the outer ear and eardrum, and produces a better sound quality.

When we speak, we hear our voices through both air conduction and bone conduction. Since bone conduction detects lower frequencies, we believe our voices are deeper than what people hear. This explains the reason our recorded voice sounds higher when it is played back. Hearing through bone conduction eliminates extraneous noise. This explains why people who are sensitive to sounds may be very loud themselves, or often hum or sing. The sounds they create are processed differently than sounds that originate outside their body. Their own sounds generate a type of white noise that filters undesirable noise.

Bone conduction hearing was discovered by the famous composer, Ludwig van Beethoven. Beethoven lost his hearing during his adult years. He experimented and found that he could hear music when biting down on a rod attached to his piano because the vibration stimulated the bones in his middle ear. The vibrations continued to the inner ear, where they were converted to electrical impulses and transmitted to the brain. Beethoven's discovery led to the creation of the bone conduction hearing aids that are widely used today.

Signs of Impaired Processing

When a person has an impaired auditory system, it affects their concentration because they cannot filter extraneous noise. The bombardment of noise impacts their behaviors and engagement in activities, which affects their ability to learn, understand instruction, or decipher important details of a conversation. The volume, pitch, frequency, and duration of the sounds also contribute to their auditory experience.

In therapy, children frequently complain about noise in school. They say that the classroom is too loud, but they can often narrow their complaints down to the sound of a particular child's voice. Their frustration might be caused by the child's tone, pitch, speech rate, or the volume at which they speak. This demonstrates that it is not only the volume that forms our experience but also the tone and pacing.

Impaired Processing in Children

Sounds can impact children in many ways, as hearing is our primary system of protection. Sounds can activate our stress response, but children lack the autonomy to control the sounds in their environment. This is the reason they display defiant behaviors and get upset easily. They are thrust into survival mode by exposure to noises. Even the anticipation of hearing a specific sound can cause them distress. The misperception about their behaviors makes the child feel anxious and lowers their self-esteem. Impaired processing also impacts their ability to understand instructions from a parent or teacher.

Life-Changing Moment...

THE GIFT STORE

Several years ago, my husband and I took the children to Vermont for a summer vacation. One afternoon, we drove up the road on Mount Mansfield, the highest mountain in Vermont. My husband pulled off at a scenic overlook. As he parked the car, he mentioned something about a gift store at the top of the trail.

He and the boys ran ahead while my daughter, Rachel, waited for me to gather my belongings. We took our time walking up the hill because I was wearing slip-on sandals, and I was carrying a purse. Several hikers passed us on the steep path; they were all wearing hiking boots, and some carried walking sticks. I joked about how funny it was that I was wearing heels, and they were all wearing the top of the line hiking gear. I can vividly recall how hard we both laughed as I stumbled on the rocks and held onto branches, saying, "You'd think they would have made this path a little easier."

At one point, an older woman leading a group of hikers down the trail stopped to admonish me. She explained that hiking is dangerous even when people have the proper gear; then, she sternly asked me why I was hiking in sandals. I said that I slipped them on because I did not realize the path to the gift store would be this steep and treacherous. The woman looked baffled, and my daughter looked at me and said, "Gift store? What gift store?" I explained that her father had said there was a gift store up there.

Rachel laughed uncontrollably. She said, "There is no gift store: you are climbing up to the peak of Mount Mansfield. Dad said there was a gift in store, referring to the view." Although we laughed as we continued up the trail, I could not stop thinking, 'How could I have misunderstood him? What is wrong with me?'

At that time, I had not learned about auditory processing; I only knew I felt foolish, like I had many times before. It was not uncommon for me to misunderstand instructions or announcements, but my hearing tests always came back normal, so people would encourage me to "pay attention."

As years passed, I learned about sensory processing. This helped me to understand why I had trouble processing auditory information. Although my hearing tests are normal, I have an auditory processing impairment that makes it hard for me to distinguish sounds when there is background noise. This is why I never heard the word 'in' that day and why other information had been previously misunderstood. This caused me to wonder if other stressful situations in life might be caused by sensory processing.

Auditory Processing Patterns

The Avoider

Avoiders are over-sensitive to noise. This causes them to steer clear of concerts, parties, or large social gatherings. They may also avoid these venues because they have difficulty tuning out background noises, making it hard for them to socialize. This explains why avoiders prefer small groups and limit the number of friends at gatherings.

Avoiders will often prefer a quiet environment, as many noises cause them to feel anxious or frustrated. Interestingly, they are often the people who hum or sing to themselves. They make their own noise because it helps to mask other sounds in the environment. They may also use noise-canceling headphones or white noise machines to reduce ambient noise.

The Bystander

The bystander does not seem to notice sounds that other people hear. They may not detect distinct sounds like water leaking or a timer that indicates dinner is ready. Therefore, it is not surprising that they do not hear the alarm clock in the morning or someone asking them a question.

Bystanders may also have a difficult time in social settings because they miss a lot of the conversation. They may also face problems in the workplace, failing to hear important announcements. In addition to these sounds, the bystander might not notice the sound of sirens approaching the intersection or footsteps creeping behind them as they walk down a dark road. Their inability to detect sounds puts them at risk and makes them appear rude if they seem to ignore someone trying to speak to them.

The Craver

Cravers have an under-sensitive system that detects sounds, but they require intense input to process them. Cravers need to hear sounds to feel content. It is not uncommon for them to have music playing in one room while watching the television in another. They set the TV or phone on the loudest volume; and they like to talk, laugh, or make mouth noises to stimulate their receptors.

Cravers do not mind noises that other people find irritating. They allow alarms to beep repeatedly, and open windows and doors to invite more noise. They enjoy the sound of a lawnmower or car engine, and they like to hear dogs barking or birds chirping. Cravers will also sing, hum, or talk to themselves to satisfy their auditory craving. They enjoy hearing sounds, but the noise can be bothersome to those around them.

The Detector

A detector will notice every noise, including an unusual hum in the computer or overhead light. They will detect subtle sounds like a thumping in a car or the buzz of a bee. Their sensitivity does not only affect their ability to hear sounds; it affects their ability to tolerate them. Many noises that cause them anxiety include sounds of chewing or sniffling.

Sounds in the workplace are distracting for detectors. People talking, phones ringing, or heels tapping down the hall interrupt their thought process. A co-worker clicking the keys on their keyboard or the sound of a squeaky chair will increase the detector's stress. The detector may attribute their frustration from these annoyances to their peers or job, but once they realize that is the sounds that are causing them stress, they can take steps to modify the environment and reduce their stress.

Calming or Arousing

Have you ever given much thought to how sounds make you feel? Many people enjoy sounds like rain, wind, or waves because they help them feel relaxed. Soft music or the hum of a fan can also be calming. Sirens, alarms, and people laughing tend to excite the nervous system. Upbeat music or a cheering crowd will arouse the nervous system, and everyday noises like appliances, motors, or running water will also impact how we feel. Therefore, it is important to recognize how sounds affect you because some reduce stress while others increase it.

POINT TO PONDER...

If chewing, whistling, humming, or tapping sounds send you into a rage, you might have a condition called Misophonia. This condition is a brain-based disorder that affects approximately 20% of the population. Noises like someone tapping on a keyboard, clicking their pen, or smacking their lips will frustrate people with misophonia, making them angry.

Researchers have discovered a physiological explanation as to why people with misophonia overreact to particular noises. Using brain scan imagery, they determined that people with misophonia process sounds differently from other people. Repetitive sounds activate their limbic system, which is the part of the brain associated with emotions, fear, and long-term memory, and this triggers a protective response.

CHAPTER 10

THE PROPRIOCEPTIVE SYSTEM

Joint & Muscle Awareness for Balance, Body Awareness, Force Production & Movement

Most people are not familiar with proprioception or the role it plays in our lives. This sense had not received much attention in the past, but people started to recognize its significance in recent years. Proprioception means 'awareness of oneself.' It detects deep pressure from receptors located throughout the body. These receptors gather information to inform us of our body's position and the muscle strength needed to lift, push, pull, or throw objects. When functioning correctly, this system plays a vital role in making us feel calm, capable, and confident.

Why Is Deep Pressure Input Important?

Proprioception is also referred to as deep pressure. It lets you always know the exact position of each body part. For example, as you read

this book, you know if your feet are crossed or flat on the floor without having to look down. You also know if your arms are bent or straight and if your fingers are together or apart, without looking at them. This system helps you control your body movements, making it possible for you to bend, stretch, run, or move around in the dark. It also lets you how much muscle strength is required to hold this book and turn each page.

Deep pressure receptors also provide information about the strength and speed with which we move our muscles. For example, when you close a door, do you exert enough power to secure it, or so much force that it slams shut? Maybe you do not use enough thrust and have to push the door over and over again until it's finally secure. Proprioception allows you to gauge your force so you can be successful.

This sense tells you how much force to use

when shaking someone's hand or when holding an item. People with an under-sensitive system might squeeze a hand too hard, and those with an over-sensitive system might have a weak handshake because they use too little force. They may also drop things more than others because their over-sensitive system is telling them they are using enough force when they need more. This demonstrates how impaired processing affects our ability to do things.

The force we exert with our muscles is detected throughout the day. We will attempt to regulate this force when throwing a ball or tossing a crumpled paper into the garbage. In these situations, we think about the amount of force to use. However, we do not typically think about muscle force when doing things like pouring a drink, opening a bag of chips, closing blinds, or scratching a mosquito bite. Proprioception is hidden in our subconscious unless something brings it to our attention.

Have you ever wondered what senses are involved in riding a bike? Deep pressure regulation plays a significant role in this activity. The deep pressure input from the pedal pressing against your foot tells you how much force you need to exert to continue riding. The tension from the handlebars pressing against your hands helps you produce a counterforce to steer the bike. The gravitational pull on your body tells you how to position your muscles to maintain your balance. This crucial information is all received and processed through your proprioceptive system. Efficient proprioceptive processing is also needed for daily activities like dressing, personal hygiene, and household chores. This sense helps you slip your legs into pants or your arms in the sleeve of a coat, without looking for the opening.

Proprioception makes it possible for you to zip your jacket or button your shirt without looking. You rely on your senses to locate the fasteners and exert the proper amount of force to complete the task. Tying your shoes, brushing your hair, and shaving are other examples of how proprioceptive feedback fosters success, but how does deep pressure input affect your emotional stability and self-esteem?

Life-Changing Moment...

THE HIDDEN POWER OF PROPRIOCEPTION

Have you ever heard of Jake Olsen or Adonis Watt? Jake was a long snapper on the University of Southern California's football team, and Adonis a running back for the Brophy College Preparatory football team. These amazing football players share many things in common; they are both young, gifted athletes, who are both blind. They lost sight at an early age, but they did not let that stop them from playing football.

Like most people, you are probably wondering how a blind person can play football. These men can play because they have learned to rely on their other senses. They depend on their well-developed sense of proprioception. They also depend on their tactile, auditory, and vestibular systems.

Proprioception is the sense that allows a quarterback to gauge how much force is needed to throw the ball accurately. It is also the sense that helps baseball players reach up to catch the ball. Proprioception enables golfers and tennis players to control their swing, and it allows soccer players to control the ball with their feet. Although proprioception is a hidden sense, it is truly one of our most amazing senses, and this is why I am excited to share this information with you today.

How Deep Pressure Input Affects Our Self-Esteem

We feel most confident when we feel capable, organized, and socially accepted. Efficient processing helps us feel this way. It helps us organize our thoughts to initiate steps to complete tasks. Good processing skills allow us to participate in group activities. This nurtures our self-esteem and fosters social acceptance. But what happens when a person has impaired processing?

One way to understand how an impaired system might feel is to think about a time your hand, arm, or foot 'fell asleep.' The peculiar sensation made that part of your body feel numb. The feeling is disorienting and unsettling. Most people stomp their feet or squeeze their arm (deep pressure activities) before trying to walk or button a shirt to regain full sensation because diminished body awareness will affect your performance and ability to succeed.

This demonstrates how an under-sensitive proprioceptive system makes a person feel incapable, disorganized, and awkward. They are then left to suffer the frustration and embarrassment that results from their inability to coordinate their movement.

POINT TO PONDER...

How does deep pressure processing contribute to anxiety? We know that efficient proprioceptive processing informs us of where our body is in space, which helps us feel calm and organized. It also allows us to move efficiently. If a person has impaired processing, it can make them feel anxious because they lack the body awareness to coordinate their movement. This leads to low self-esteem and anxiety.

The wonderful news is that deep pressure input can produce a sense of calm that lasts for hours. This is why weighted blankets have become so popular. They provide substantial proprioceptive input to many proprioceptive receptors.

How The Proprioceptive System Works

This system receives information from stretch and pressure receptors located in our skin, muscles, ligaments, and joints. Input from surrounding tissue also provides information about our body's position, orientation, and movement. This sense also receives data from receptors located in our inner ear, which detect motion and direction.

Subconscious detection means that we do not have to think about our body position or the force of our muscle movement unless something draws our attention to it. For instance, if we pick-up an empty shampoo bottle instead of our full one, we quickly notice that it feels lighter. Proprioception feedback tells us it was empty based on the weight. These receptors also tell us that more muscle strength is required to

lift canned goods than paper products when carrying groceries. Apart from noticeable differences that draw our attention to muscle force, we do not consciously think about our body's position or the amount of muscle force being exerted.

We stimulate our proprioceptive system every time we move. Each time we lean, bend, stand, or sit down, we stimulate these receptors. They are also stimulated when we exercise, chew gum, or bite our fingernails.

POINT TO PONDER...

Proprioceptive feedback provides us with a detailed road map of our bodies. It lets us know the exact location and position of each body part. This plays a crucial role in our confidence, abilities, and success. This is one of the reasons we feel relaxed and secure after sitting in a pool or bath. The water provides isometric pressure to receptors across our body, making us feel capable and relaxed.

Did you know that sitting in a bath or pool could make you feel more organized and capable? This is why I wrote this book. Awareness of these reactions is knowledge that you can use to conquer anxiety and stress on a daily basis.

provides foundational support to our other senses to achieve success.

It would not be easy to coordinate movement when the proprioceptive system is not functioning correctly. Proprioception determines the required force to do things safely, like carrying a pot of boiling water, pushing a baby stroller, or shaving. It also determines the strength and movement needed to brush our hair, scrub our body, or pet our dog. Nearly everything we do requires good proprioceptive processing skills.

Impaired Processing in Children

Impaired processing causes many problems for children. Some children crave movement and deep pressure, causing them to run around and bump into things. Other children might bang their heads, pull their hair, or jump off furniture. Their actions are often rough and forceful because they are unable to control the force of their muscles. These children can also appear weak or slothful. Whether they are under- or over-sensitive to this sensation, they will each face difficulties caused by impaired processing.

Children who have an under-sensitive system are misunderstood. They get in trouble for hitting or pushing other children because they cannot control their muscle force. The child who has an over-sensitive system will also have problems regulating their force. Their sensitivity causes them to drop things and or have trouble tying their shoes or manipulating fasteners on

Signs of Impaired Processing

Have you ever needed to do a chore, but did not know where to begin? You had to stop and think about what to do to complete the task. Our ability to organize thoughts and initiate action relies on efficient proprioceptive processing. Impaired processing affects body awareness and motor planning skills. Proprioception plays a crucial role in fostering these skills and clothes. They will also have difficulty opening a milk carton, a bag of chips, or closing the zipper on their backpacks. These youngsters drift into a daydream when seated and appear uncoordinated in gym class because they lack body awareness.

Life-Changing Moment...

THEY ALWAYS FALL DOWN

One day a young boy came to therapy in tears. He was told he could no longer play tag with his classmates. He said, "I do what they do. I tag the other kids, but they always fall down." This child was not able to gauge the appropriate amount of force needed to tag the other children. His nervous system did not register the pressure until he pushed with enough power to detect it. His inability to modulate proprioception input resulted in social isolation.

He was excluded from group activities, including invitations to birthday parties. He could not understand why he was always in trouble. As a result, he suffered from anxiety and low self-esteem. This happens when people are not educated about proprioception and sensory processing. They assume the rough behavior is intentional.

After this little boy received sensory therapy, he was able to gauge his muscle strength more accurately. His mother said that upon learning about sensory processing and how his behaviors resulted from inefficient processing, everything changed. She said that the awareness alone brought about change and that after receiving therapy, her son is now happy, assertive, and confident. Therefore, I believe it is so important for every person to learn about the senses and sensory processing. This awareness is truly life changing.

> ## POINT TO PONDER...
>
> Everyone processes proprioceptive information differently. Some people can tolerate a lot of input, while others cannot tolerate even the smallest amount. People who crave deep pressure will prefer specific types of encounters. Some might prefer the continuous pressure from a weighted blanket, while others may choose intermittent stimulation produced by running or jumping. The type of input that satisfies a sensory craving is based on personal preference. People should try out different kinds of sensory experiences to determine the ones that meet their sensory needs.

Proprioceptive Processing Patterns

The Avoider

Avoiders are overly sensitive to proprioceptive input. They limit movement that stimulates their receptors, preferring sedentary activities like reading or watching TV. They may also appear to be clumsy or careless because they perceive the slightest input as adequate when holding or lifting items. This causes them to drop things or knock them over. They also have trouble opening jars, water bottles, or snack bags because it is hard for them to regulate their muscle force production.

Avoiders may also refuse to eat hard or chewy foods because these types of food provide too much stimulation to the receptors in their jaw. They limit their diet to foods they can tolerate, giving the impression they are fussy people.

The Bystander

The bystander has an under-sensitive system that does not detect the amount of proprioceptive input necessary for movement, body awareness, and muscle force. Their actions are slow and uncoordinated, making them appear lazy and disorganized. Bystanders might be clumsy and inattentive. They may stomp their feet or saunter when walking and spill drinks when pouring because they lack muscle force control.

If you have a bystander in the house, you will likely hear reminders for them to 'hurry or get moving' because bystanders have difficulty coordinating their movement. Their diminished sense can make it hard for them to get showered and dressed. If self-care requires this much effort, we can understand why it could be difficult to do more complex tasks.

The Craver

Cravers have an under-sensitive system that prompts them to seek out deep pressure input. This is the reason they frequently stomp their feet or slam items when putting them down;

they need intense input to sense it. Cravers tend to use too much force when doing things, which causes them to move about their environment carelessly.

Cravers often enjoy aerobics, yoga, running, and weight training because these activities activate stretch and pressure receptors that arouse their nervous system while providing a feeling of contentment. For some, these endeavors do not provide enough input, which prompts them to seek out more risky activities like bungee jumping, cliff diving, or motocross racing.

Cravers prefer heavy blankets to get a good night's sleep. They like to wear heavy boots, hats, and tight-fitting clothing throughout the day. They also tap their feet, cross their arms, or chew gum because these provide input, which is calming and organizing.

The Detector

A detector notices deep pressure stimulation more than the bystander and craver. This impacts their ability to perform tasks efficiently. When doing things like dancing, they may move to the left when everyone else moves to the right, and they might clap off-beat. Their lack of coordination can make it hard for them to pace their movement.

Detectors can be very particular about the clothes they wear and the items they use. It is not uncommon for them to have a favorite mug, pen, or blanket. Their preferences, sensitivity, and lack of tolerance limit their ability to be adaptable to change.

> ## POINT TO PONDER...
>
> Safety and self-esteem are two of the main concerns associated with an impaired proprioceptive system. Impairments affect a person's ability to gauge the muscle force necessary to lift and carry heavy or hot items. It also makes it hard to regulate force when spanking a child or petting an animal. This can lead to a safety issue.

An impaired system can make a person feel incapable, clumsy, or inadequate, which lowers their self-esteem. Children who crave deep pressure are often misunderstood. Their behaviors subject them to discipline or embarrassment, affecting their self-image.

Calming or Arousing

Why do so many people enjoy massages, hugs, a heavy blanket, or being cuddled? It is because the deep pressure stimulates the proprioceptive receptors, which makes them feel safe and calm. This is why people tense their muscles, clench their fists or stomp their feet when upset. The deep pressure helps them to calm down. Chewing gum or sucking on hard candy can also relax us because they provide stimulation to receptors on the jaw.

These activities, along with exercising, yoga, wrestling, or dancing, can have a soothing effect. The proprioceptive input from swimming also provides isometric pressure that is relaxing. Daily activities will also provide input, like walking up and downstairs, carrying the laundry, pulling a door open, or lifting our cell phones. This increases body awareness, producing a sense of calm.

As you learn more about each sensory system, you should be able to identify activities that are arousing or calming. This will help you determine which inputs make you feel organized and focused, and which ones are arousing.

CHAPTER 11

THE OLFACTORY SYSTEM

Detects different types of odors and scents

The olfactory system is responsible for our sense of smell. It is 10,000 times more sensitive than any other sense, and it helps us identify people, places, objects, and foods. It also identifies noxious odors that warn us of danger.

Olfaction plays a critical role in our survival. It detects odors throughout the day and night, even while we are sleeping. This sense not only helps us identify odors; it also plays a crucial role in creating the flavor of food. Our taste buds detect the taste of food. This combines with food odors to properly determine the flavor of food. Therefore, food does not taste as flavorful when you have a stuffy nose.

The olfactory system also plays a vital role in creating emotional memories. This explains how the smell of fresh-baked cookies can bring you back to your mother's kitchen. Our sense of smell is unique because it bypasses the cortex of the brain and is routed directly through the limbic system. The limbic system is the portion of the brain that processes our emotions, motivation, and long-term memories. This explains how familiar scents elicit memories and emotions.

It is not only a pleasant fragrance that creates treasured memories. For some people, the smell of gasoline reminds them of memorable times working on a motor with their father. For others, the smell of chlorine brings back memories of playing in a pool. Like evergreen, gingerbread, or pumpkin pie, fragrances associated with the holidays elicit pleasurable memories for most people. However, for others, these odors could trigger thoughts of their painful past.

The food industry is aware of how aromas

influence our feelings and use enticing aromas to increase sales. Since our sense of smell is heightened when we are hungry, it makes it hard for us to resist the smell of cinnamon buns, fried chicken, or other tasty foods. Dunkin Donuts once conducted a research study to determine how the aroma of coffee influences consumer spending. They sprayed a coffee scent on commuter buses in South Korea, hoping this would market their products in a fun and engaging way. Their coffee spray, known as 'Flavor Radio,' proved to be quite successful. The locations along the commuter line recorded a 29% increase in sales during this marketing campaign. The rich aroma made it hard for the consumer to resist buying coffee at the next stop; however, it is not only the food industry that capitalizes on our sense of smell.

Many businesses use scents to influence customer behavior. Upscale hotels spray fragrances to create pleasurable memories, and casinos release odors that have been shown to increase consumer gambling by over 50%. Retail stores and restaurants also use various scents to increase their profits. Our sense of smell influences our spending habits, memories, and the flavor of foods, but they also impact many other areas of our lives. Studies show that body odor is an aphrodisiac in some countries, yet body odors are considered repulsive in others. Whether we detect a natural odor or an aromatic scent, our perception of other people is influenced by smell.

Bad breath can also be offensive. Since there is no politically correct way to inform someone of their malodor, it leaves no option other than to avoid them. Offensive odors can significantly affect a person's social, professional, and personal relationships because foul odors prompt people to distance themselves from the offensive source.

How Odors Affect Us

Research has found that the scent of lavender, coffee, and vanilla each helps reduce stress. The smell of lemon oil or peppermint has been shown to increase attention, focus, and productivity, and nightmares can be kept away by spraying a flowery scent in the bedroom before going to sleep. Surprisingly, smells like citrus have been shown to alter our perception of another person's appearance. For example, participants estimated people's weight to be as much as five pounds lighter when a citrus smell was present. Undeniably, odors affect many areas of our lives. This explains why aromatherapy has become so popular.

We experience all types of scents throughout the day. We smell things like body odors, cleaning products, air fresheners, and foods. We also detect natural odors like grass, trees, and flowers. We experience a multitude of fragrances that are impacting our lives. Odors can even trigger PTSD. Smells may also limit a person's diet if they refuse to eat foods that have a strong or offensive odor. The smell may cause them to gag or vomit.

Anxiety, pregnancy, and certain medical conditions can also alter our perception of odors. These conditions can cause typically pleasant fragrances to smell bad.

Odors have a profound effect on our lives. In therapy, I have witnessed children who are normally unable to interact socially suddenly engage and become talkative when a specific scent was introduced. I have also seen children calmed during meltdowns when given an item with that same berry scent. It is always intriguing to learn how fragrances impact our behaviors and how they can be used to improve our lives. Sensory awareness is truly life changing.

POINT TO PONDER...

Can odors affect a person's social acceptance? Absolutely because there is no politically correct way to tell someone that they smell. Therefore, people distance themselves from those who have an offensive odor. Foul odors do not go unnoticed, whether they come from your breath, body, shoes, or clothing. Scents will influence people's perceptions of you, which can impede your social inclusion.

How The Olfactory System Works

A smell is created by an odor molecule that enters through the nostrils and adheres to the tissue that covers the back of the nasal cavity. The molecule dissolves in the mucus and attaches to the end of one of the 40-plus million olfactory receptors. Each receptor can only detect one kind of odorant, similar to a lock and key. Once a receptor is stimulated, it sends an electrical impulse to the brain that interprets the specific odor.

Once a scent is detected, the potency decreases to half its original strength within 4 minutes. The intensity also weakens after repeated exposure. This explains why we can hardly smell the perfume we applied minutes earlier, or why we cannot smell a scented candle after burning for a while.

Signs of Impaired Processing

An impaired olfactory system can impact a person's ability to detect noxious odors, putting them in harm's way. An under-sensitive system may not notice smells that warn of danger, like smoke or rotting food. These smells activate our survival mode to keep us safe. An under-sensitive olfactory system will also impact the flavor of food, causing people to restrict their diet.

People who have an over-sensitive system may avoid places because of the smell experience. Their over-sensitivity can also impede their ability to maintain a healthy diet because of their inability to tolerate food odors.

Impaired Processing in Children

Children face the same challenges the adults face when their olfactory system is impaired. The only difference is that children lack the autonomy to restrict or avoid their exposure to odors. Intolerance to odors could affect their engagement in school and emotional stability.

Children who are over-sensitive to odors may not tolerate the smell of cleaning products, the bathroom, or the lunchroom at school. They may also be bothered by the scent of their schoolmates' clothes, shoes, or snacks. Over-sensitive children may not be able to tolerate the smell of a person or the odors in someone's house. They may avoid parks or stores because they detect smells that are offensive to them. When they are exposed to foul odors, they may become angry and aggressive. Sensory overload may also occur when they attend birthday parties or other large social gatherings where they encounter different scents.

Children who have an under-sensitive system may not detect the pleasant fragrances of nature or the appetite-stimulating aroma of dinner cooking. They also may fail to notice an offense odor from their shoes, or clothing that alerts them to change to clean clothes. These children are also in danger of missing the protective odors that warn them of fire or spoiled food.

Olfactory Processing Patterns

The Avoider

The avoider has an over-sensitive olfactory system that detects odors that other people cannot smell. Avoiders prefer unscented products, and they do not care for most air fresheners, scented candles, or essential oils. They are bothered by the smell of certain foods, going so far as to distance themselves from someone who is eating an aromatic meal or refusing to go to certain eateries because of the smell. Their over-sensitivity also causes them to limit their diet due to food odors.

The Bystander

"You can't smell that?" is a question the bystander will often hear. Their under-sensitive system does not detect odors that most people notice. They may not smell rotting food in the trash can or the eggs burning in the pan. Their under-sensitivity can become hazardous if they are unable to smell smoke, sour milk, or rotting food. They might also overlook the smell of a gas leak or the smell of something burning, putting them in harm's way.

People may assume that having a diminished sense of smell is good because the bystander does not have to experience repulsive odors; however, they do not experience pleasant scents either. They may not smell cookies baking in the oven or the salty air at the beach. Imagine how different life would be if you could not smell coffee brewing or tomato sauce simmering. Scents and fragrances enhance our world. They create memories, bring us pleasure, and help to keep us safe.

The Craver

People who crave scents have an under-sensitive olfactory system. They detect odors but require a higher intensity to process the fragrance. This is the reason that cravers like to use perfumes, scented products, or aromatherapy. They also open windows to allow the essence of nature to fill the air. They enjoy the smell of leaves burning, freshly cut grass, or the chlorine from the pool, and it is not uncommon for them to smell things like lotions or soaps before using them.

The Detector

The detector has an over-sensitive system that detects most odors. They are always aware of smells in the air and monitor their ability to tolerate them. There are many scents that a detector enjoys and equally as many that they despise. They are quick to notice new smells as well as differences or changes in a familiar scent.

Calming or Arousing

It is crucial to recognize the effect that odors can have on you. Some fragrances arouse the nervous system, while others calm it down. Aromatherapy, which has become increasingly popular over the past several years, is the therapeutic use of essential oils extracted from plants. Essential oils can increase energy, productivity, and sex appeal. They can also be used to reduce stress, improve sleep, and help people lose weight.

Aromachology is the study of how scents influence human behavior. It collects scientific data under controlled conditions to determine how fragrances affect a person's emotions, mood, or temperament. This research has provided a wealth of information about the powerful influence of scents. For example, the benefits from the smell of lavender have been touted for years. People claim it reduces emotional stress, which is why many products are infused with this fragrance. Lavender scented pillows, blankets, and bath products are available in most stores. A flowery scent called Ylang Ylang is used by people to feel more relaxed. Vanilla is used to reduce stress, and studies show it can make a person more socially appealing. The smell of cedar reduces tension, while the scent of frankincense reduces depression or anxiety. Jasmine or lavender can improve the quality of sleep, and some claim that lavender helps people fall asleep faster.

Some scents increase a person's energy. They include lemon, lime, grapefruit, orange, peppermint, spearmint, cinnamon, or coffee. Rosemary improves memory, and the smell of green apples, peppermint, or bananas helps people lose weight.

We continually encounter scents that impact our cognitive skills and physical well-being. People should never underestimate the power of smells, nor discount them as a source of anxiety. The more you understand how odors are processed in our brain, the easier it will be to manage scent encounters.

CHAPTER 12

THE GUSTATORY SYSTEM

Detects taste through receptors located on the tongue

The gustatory system is responsible for detecting the five basic taste sensations: sweet, salty, sour, bitter, and umami (savory). Our ability to taste protects us from ingesting things that could be harmful to our bodies. Taste also helps to arouse or calm the nervous system. Sour or spicy foods can energize us, while sweet or salty foods tend to be calming.

Taste is just one of the many senses that contribute to our experience of eating. As we eat, our olfactory system detects the smell of food, while the auditory system detects the sound of the food's crunch. This helps us determine if the fruit, cracker, or vegetable is fresh or stale. Our tactile system identifies the texture of foods, and our proprioceptive system gauges the amount of force necessary to bite and chew our foods.

Many factors influence the flavor of foods. For example, studies found that the temperature of food affects the way it tastes. Participants reported that ham tasted saltier when served cold, beer tasted more bitter when served warm, and the bitter taste of coffee intensified as the coffee cooled down to room temperature.

Sweet foods taste sweeter when they are warm. Cold decreases the intensity of sweetness, explaining why melted ice cream tastes too sweet to enjoy. Studies have also found that drinking ice-cold water before you eat makes sweetened foods taste less sweet. They also discovered that the taste of sour food is intensified when served at room temperature compared to being served at a hot or cold temperature.

A stuffy nose will decrease the flavor of

foods, while nausea intensifies it. Age, pregnancy, smoking, medication, obesity, and other health conditions can also affect the taste. Hunger makes us more sensitive to sweet and salty foods. This is the reason we seek out these foods when feeling hungry. Interestingly, studies have also found that what we hear while eating alters our perception of taste. Listening to low tones will create a different impression of flavor than when hearing high-frequency sounds.

POINT TO PONDER...

Did you know that the way you eat meals impacts the taste of foods? For example, if you eat your steak without switching to a side dish after 3 to 4 mouthfuls, your taste buds adapt to the steak's flavor, and it will not taste as savory. To intensify the flavor of foods, you should eat a small amount of one food followed by a few mouthfuls of another. Switching between foods intensifies the flavor.

How The Gustatory System Works

The gustatory system receives information through chemical receptors located on the tongue, the lining of the cheeks, and the roof of the mouth. These receptors detect the food's

taste to determine if they are sweet, sour, salty, and bitter or umami (savory). The perception of how food tastes starts when food mixes with saliva on our taste buds. As we chew, the food odors stimulate the olfactory nerve (smell). The taste and odor information is sent to the brain where the flavor of the food is constructed.

How Foods Affect Us

Eating sweet foods causes our brain to produce the feel-good chemical, dopamine. Overconsumption of sugary foods results in dopamine flooding, which can lead to food addiction. This occurs when the brain starts to require more sugar to attain the same level of pleasure. Eliminating sweets from our diet can cause a 'sugar crash.' This results in fatigue, weakness, nervousness, and anxiety, along with many other physical symptoms.

We crave sweet foods because they produce dopamine. They arouse the nervous system, helping us to feel energized and alert. These foods can also have a calming effect by increasing our pleasure after we eat them. And we find salty foods to be enticing because they stimulate the brain's reward system. Spicy foods arouse the nervous system by stimulating pain receptors. This causes the brain to produce chemicals like dopamine and endorphins to block the pain and this creates a feeling of euphoria. This is why some people experience a 'runner's high' from eating spicy foods. Spicy foods will also speed up our metabolism, increasing our circulation and body temperature.

Historically, a bitter taste indicated that a food source might be toxic. This taste warned our early ancestors that a food source could be poisonous. Today we know that many bitter foods are safe for eating and provide health benefits, like regulating blood sugar and hunger. Brussel sprouts, greens, and grapefruit are examples of bitter foods that can lower our cancer risk and increase our hearts' health. The three most common bitter foods consumed today are coffee, chocolate, and beer, though the first two are frequently sweetened for flavor.

Crunchy foods can be quite alerting. The deep pressure required to eat these foods provides proprioceptive input and increases blood flow to the brain. Eating crunchy foods draws attention to your mouth. It also produces bone conduction sound that serves as a 'white noise' that masks other sounds as you chew. People are drawn to crunchy foods because they associate the crunch factor with the freshness.

Cold food like ice cream, can arouse our nervous system, while hot foods and drinks produce a calming effect. Many foods can be both calming and alerting. For example, an ice pop's cold temperature can be alerting, and the sucking motion to eat it can be calming.

Foods with mixed textures, like yogurt with granola and fruit, can be a sensory nightmare for some people. A person may like the foods individually, but the combination of textures and flavors may cause a gustatory or tactile overload. There are so many variables to consider when it comes to foods: the flavor, texture, smell, and the force required to chew it.

POINT TO PONDER...

Oral stimulation has been shown to improve attention when used in therapy. As part of a sensory diet, I will sometimes give my clients an ice pop as part of their sensory diet. The icy treat helps the children increase their attention and self-regulation. Impulsive children who refuse to listen or follow instructions have also shown improvement after eating an ice pop. The oral input helps them to calm down and follow instructions.

Interestingly, these same results were not achieved when the children were given a lollipop. This indicates that the cold temperature or the ice pop's liquid played a significant role in the behavioral changes. This clinical observation validated that oral stimulation improves attention and self-regulation.

Oral-Motor Skills

Eating requires efficient oral-motor coordination. Oral-motor skills include biting, chewing, and sucking on foods. Chewing is alerting because it provides proprioceptive input and increases blood flow to the brain.

Chewing gum can significantly affect our mood, mental performance, and stress. It produces similar amounts of blood flow to the brain as mild exercise. It has also been shown to reduce levels of cortisol, the stress hormone. Studies have found that the benefits of chewing gum lasted approximately twenty minutes.

Chewing also produces a calming effect while helping to increase focus. It provides deep pressure input to the jaw. This explains why some people bite their fingernails or chew on their pens. Educators are now recognizing the benefits of chewing and are allowing children to chew gum or eat foods during class.

food. Interestingly, they all completed their assignments on-time without any signs of avoidance or stress. They also displayed significant improvement with concentration and accuracy.

When asked for their feedback, they reported that the flavors and chewing helped them attend and relax. They also stated that having control over what food they could eat helped reduce their anxiety. This clinical observation established that oral inputs can be used to reduce anxiety and increase concentration.

POINT TO PONDER...

In therapy, we will sometimes use food as part of a sensory diet. We presented a group of teenagers who suffered from anxiety, with a selection of sweet, sour, chewy, crunchy, and salty foods. We notified the group that they could eat any of these foods while working on a difficult school assignment.

As they worked, some children sampled several different types of foods, while others chose to eat only one

Signs of Impaired Processing

People who have an over or under-sensitive gustatory system limit their diet to a few food choices. The person who has an over-sensitive system may avoid different types of foods or flavors, and they may gag on foods that overwhelm them. They might also be overly sensitive to the texture of foods.

If a person has an under-sensitive gustatory system, they may limit foods that seem bland. They prefer savory or spicy foods that stimulate their taste receptors, so they frequently add spices or hot sauce to meals to make them palpable. The under-sensitive person will seek out foods with intense flavor like sour, peppery, salty cuisines, and sweet or bitter foods. They may also suck on hard candies or chew gum to stimulate their gustatory system.

Impaired Processing in Children

Like adults, children who have an over-sensitive gustatory system restrict their diet. They may also gag or have trouble swallowing certain foods. This could impact their development if they are unable to maintain a healthy, nutritious diet. Their dietary restrictions might also affect their social engagement because eating is often a part of social gatherings.

The children who have an under-sensitive gustatory system may exhibit unusual behaviors. They might lick or chew on inedible objects to experience taste sensations. They may also bite or mouth things, including their shirt collar, zipper, or hair. These children may not be willing to try new foods but prefer intense tastes to stimulate their system. Some children pocket food in their mouths or drool due to their under-sensitive system.

Oral Fixations

Why do some people chew gum, smoke cigarettes, or bite their lips? People who have an oral fixation have an unconscious obsession with having something in their mouth. They like to chew, suck, or nibble on things. They may also talk excessively or display unusual mouth movements. Oral stimulation provides an outlet for nervous energy, but what causes oral fixations?

Most research reflects Freud's psychosexual development theory and oral fixation; however, sensory therapists feel these behaviors are due to a sensory imbalance. The cravings may be caused by an under-sensitive gustatory system that is seeking stimulation. An oral fixation might also be caused by an under-sensitive tactile or proprioceptive system that needs more input.

Research suggests that oral fixations are learned behaviors. When we consider the fact that we were given pacifiers and bottles from infancy to comfort us, it is reasonable to assume that our brain established a connection between oral stimulation and stress reduction.

There is also research that suggests a nutritional imbalance is to blame. These studies have found that iron deficiency can lead to unusual eating or oral habits. Regardless of the underlying cause, an occupational therapist can provide sensory strategies to reduce the behaviors.

Oral fixations in adults are often satisfied with unhealthy behaviors. Some people bite their lips, inside their cheek, or bite their fingernails. Many people will bite their pen caps or straws, and some will even put small hard objects in their mouths and push them around using their tongue and teeth. These might include paper clips, bottle caps, or toothpicks, all of which pose a safety risk. Chewing tobacco, cigars, pipes, or cigarettes are unhealthy options used to satisfy an oral craving. People will also use beverages and foods to satisfy their oral craving. And in some instances, people will grind their teeth to relieve stress through deep pressure to the oral cavity.

Some children explore the world with their mouths. They will eat paste or glue sticks as a means of understanding things in their environment. They mouth, bite, and eat inedible objects to satisfy their sensory craving. These behaviors have prompted the creation of safe, chewable items like chewable pencil toppers or bracelets. Oral cravings might also be satisfied by providing different types of oral input like blowing through straws, sucking on an ice pop, or sucking a very thick shake through a straw. A vibrating toothbrush or vibrating chew toy may also help some children.

Behavioral strategies that include a positive reward system can also help children become aware of their chewing habits. Parents can increase the child's awareness of oral behaviors by introducing an alternate action. For instance, each time the child bites or chews on something inappropriate, the parent instructs the child to go to the sink and rinse their mouth. The sensation from the water stimulates their oral cavity and increases their awareness to help break the habit. Many families have found good results from implementing these strategies.

Gustatory Processing Patterns

The Avoider

The avoider has an over-sensitive gustatory system. They cannot tolerate intense flavors like spicy or sour foods. They are also particular about their food's texture and avoid edibles that are too mushy, wet, dry, hard, or crunchy. Their inability to tolerate foods can also impact their social inclusion as foods are often a part of social gatherings.

The Bystander

The bystander has an under-sensitive system, which makes it hard for them to detect tastes. They like to try new foods, and they seem to have a limitless diet. They might eat hot peppers or very spicy foods, failing to notice the potency of the flavors. This could put them at risk of harm if they continue to eat foods that could irritate their skin. They may also fail to notice if a food is too hot or too cold, exposing them to further danger.

The Craver

Show me a person who smokes and drinks, and I'll show you a gustatory craver. Cravers have an under-sensitive system that needs intense oral stimulation to feel content. They may crave chewing tobacco, cigarettes, cigars, or alcoholic beverages because the intense flavor helps satisfy their gustatory craving. Cravers usually prefer savory foods: the spicier, the better. They tend to like foods that are heavily seasoned and will often add hot sauce to meals. Cravers might not only enjoy an unrestricted diet; they may eat unusual foods that make most people cringe. They might also bite their fingernails, chew on a straw, and crunch on ice, or they like to have a mint, candy, or gum in their mouth.

The Detector

The detector has an over-sensitive gustatory system that causes them to limit their diet. They might try new foods but limit their selections based on taste, texture, and temperature. The detector is more or less, a picky eater. They notice the slightest change in flavors. They may refuse to eat cookies, cereals, or other products if it is not their favorite brand. Once they find a flavor that they like, they have a hard time accepting variations.

POINT TO PONDER...

Have you ever watched the World Series? If so, you may have noticed that many players chew on gum or chewing tobacco. Sometimes, they gnaw on their glove or shirt or take a mouthful of water only to spit it out. They seek out oral stimulation because it helps them reduce stress and increase their focus.

Calming or Arousing

Have you ever given much thought to how foods affect you? They can help you relax, or they can energize you. Typically, spicy, sour, or bitter tasting foods stimulate the nervous system, but these foods can also produce a calming effect. Crunchy or chewy foods can also be arousing and calming. It is important for you to start to recognize the effect that these foods have on you.

Hot foods and beverages have a calming effect, while cold foods tend to be more alerting. Sweet and salty foods are considered comfort foods because they help reduce stress while sucking hard candies or chewing gum can be either calming or alerting. These are just some brief examples of how foods can rouse us when we need energy or calm us when we feel stressed.

CHAPTER 13

THE INTEROCEPTIVE SYSTEM

*Detects information about our physical condition
from receptors located within our body*

The interoceptive system refers to our inner senses. This system receives information about our physical condition from various internal receptors. It detects things like hunger, thirst, pain, body temperature, respiration, and sleepiness in addition to other sensations like sexual arousal, nausea, or the need to use the bathroom. It is important to develop an understanding of the inner senses because, as our external senses, the inner senses can be either under- or over-sensitive. Under- or over-sensitivity can affect a person's emotional regulation and overall well-being, much like an imbalance in our external senses.

Hunger is one of the well-known inner senses that affects people's temperament. It can cause people to become irritable, which is why people now use the term 'hangry' to describe a person whose personality is altered by hunger. People also behave differently when they are thirsty, overtired, overheated, nauseous, or have to use the bathroom.

Many inner senses help shape our lives. For instance, intuition, motivation, decision-making, and problem-solving are part of our interoceptive system. Emotional regulation, reading gestures, understanding norms, and sense of time are also some of the factors controlled by interoceptive center of the brain. These senses are discussed in greater detail in the Life Changers Sensory Solutions Program section of the book.

Like our external senses, the inner senses can increase stress when there is an imbalance. Unfortunately, we cannot manipulate the inner senses as easily as we can our external ones. We can satisfy our hunger, thirst, or sexual desires, but we cannot easily regulate others like our metabolism or heart rate. However, it is important to recognize how inner senses can contribute to our daily stress.

Signs of Impaired Processing

There are far too many inner senses to discuss at this time; however, some require our consideration. If a person has an under-sensitive system that fails to detect hunger or thirst, that person may not be appropriately nourished or hydrated. This can affect their physical and cognitive abilities. Some medical conditions affect sensory processing, such as Alzheimer's or traumatic brain injury. These can affect a person's ability to recognize hunger, thirst, or satiety, and may impact other areas of their lives.

Sensory processing impairments can also impact a sense of sexual gratification. A person might not have any sex drive or have an overactive one. An inability to regulate sexual arousal could result in risky, unhealthy behaviors and make someone vulnerable to sex addiction.

Sleep is another inner sense that can have a significant impact on our behaviors. A lack of restful sleep reduces our attentiveness and diminishes our reaction time. Over forty percent of Americans are reportedly sleep deprived. This explains why driver fatigue is one of the leading causes of car accidents. Sleeping too much can also become a problem.

An under-sensitive system may also fail to notice if the body is overheating on a hot, summer day. This insensitivity could result in a heat stroke. Temperature dysregulation can also put a person at risk of hypothermia if they are unable to detect that their body is getting too cold in freezing temperatures. Dysregulation can also make it difficult to adjust from one temperature to another.

There are countless ways that interoception processing can impact our lives, including our ability to notice pain. Pain is a protective mechanism that informs us if we are ill, injured, or in danger of a medical episode. It alerts us that there is a problem so we can take corrective action. An under-sensitive system may fail to detect these warning signals, and an over-sensitive system may misidentify minor injuries as potential danger.

These inner senses also regulate laughter and excitement. If a person has an over-sensitive system, they may laugh easily or have difficulty controlling their enthusiasm. They might even cry more easily than others. If a person's system is under-sensitive, they may need prompting to smile or laugh. These are just some examples of how sensory processing from inner senses can affect our actions and behaviors.

Therapeutic Application

I trust that by now you have a better understanding of how your amazing senses affect your life. This awareness will empower you to make subtle changes that will reduce your stress. However, to reap the full benefits of this sensory education, you need to learn how to apply this knowledge to your everyday life.

The next section of the book includes the Life Changers Sensory Solutions Program. This self-development program includes the same exercises used by therapists in professional practice. Each module simulates the format of a professional therapy session, allowing you to enjoy the benefits of sensory-based therapy from the comfort of your home. The therapeutic activities have been carefully designed to facilitate ease of use by providing templates to structure your responses.

I strongly encourage you to complete each exercise, even if you think the topic does not apply to you. There is a gem of wisdom in each activity that is sure to change your life. The investment of your time to complete this program will surely give you a life-long return on your investment.

THE LIFE CHANGERS SENSORY SOLUTIONS PROGRAM

WELCOME TO THE LIFE CHANGERS SENSORY SOLUTIONS PROGRAM

This unique self-help program teaches you how to reduce your anxiety and increase your self-esteem from the comfort of your own home. It includes the same therapeutic activities I use in practice to teach my clients how they can enjoy a successful, stress-free life. In each of the twelve sessions, I included educational instruction and real-life analogies to guide you through the exercises.

The activities are designed to teach you how to identify stressors that are adversely affecting your life. You will also learn to recognize how sensory encounters alter your brain chemistry. This knowledge will change your life. It will empower you to take control of stressful situations so you can enjoy the stress-free life you deserve.

I am confident this curriculum will provide solutions for managing your anxiety. It will also help you understand other people's behaviors, making you more aware so you can become a more compassionate partner, parent, employee, or friend.

If you prefer guided assistance to complete this program, please visit **www.SensoryAuthority.com** to review available options.

SENSATIONAL YOU

sn't it exciting to learn more about yourself and how sensory processing shapes your life? The processing patterns that you identified earlier establish the foundation of your sensory profile. In this session, you will continue developing your sensory profile by identifying specific situations that trigger stress. You will also increase your sensory awareness by characterizing sensory encounters by likes and dislikes.

SESSION GOALS:

☐ Review the Sensory Profile exercise completed earlier and indicate your results on the *Sensory Profile Summary*.

☐ Complete the *Self-Reflection Assessment* to identify situations that contribute to your stress. This activity will help you identify patterns in the sensory events that cause you distress.

☐ Complete the *Sensory Preference Assessment*. This will help you identify sensory experiences that increase the feel-good chemicals in your brain.

☐ Complete the *Sensory Challenge Assessment* to identify the sensory experiences that increase stress producing chemicals in your brain.

Please visit **http://www.SensoryAuthority.com/reader-bonus** to download additional copies of the therapeutic exercises contained in this book.

Life-Changing Moment...

THE RELATIVES ARE COMING

You just found out that the relatives are coming to visit. It is not that you don't want to see everyone; it's just that these visits never go well. You start to feel anxious because you are going to have to 'deal' with having company. It may seem like you don't enjoy being around other people, but that may not be the reason you feel upset when the relatives come to visit.

These visits create stress because your normally tranquil home transforms into a loud house full of guests. You try to engage in conversation, but the competing sounds are too hard to filter out, so all you hear is loud, irritating noise. It might also be that when the relatives come over, special meals are served, and you do not like to try new foods, nor do you care for the way these foods smell.

When the relatives visit, you may not be able to sit in your favorite chair, the only one that you find comfortable. This forces you to retreat to a hard, uncomfortable piece of furniture. You also cannot listen to your playlist or watch your favorite TV shows. The TV might be turned on, but it's only creating more noise. There will also be different scents from perfumes and body odors, making this experience overwhelming.

When the relatives visit, there is also a lot of hugging or kissing. This means you'll be exposed to different types of touch, and people might bump into you because the house is so crowded. If you are sensitive to touch, this will make you feel anxious. You may wish you could leave, but that would be rude.

This scenario illustrates how sensory encounters can feel like an assault or a violation. Many of us can relate to this experience. It demonstrates how subtle, seemingly unimportant sensory experiences like sitting in a favorite chair or eating familiar foods are an undervalued comfort.

It also reveals how situations, including touch encounters, hearing too many sounds, or a lack of control, produce anxiety. The stress may cause you to yell, curse, or withdraw from others. You might also express your frustration by throwing things or stomping your feet, all because... the relatives are coming to visit. However, even with all the stressors, you can still do some sensory activities to help lessen the negative aspects and enjoy your relatives more.

SENSORY PROFILE SUMMARY

Complete the chart below, indicating the processing pattern that you identified earlier for each of your senses. Remember, a person can display one processing pattern for a sense or display a combination of patterns. For example, a person can be a detector that avoids input more than craves it or a detector that craves input more than avoids it. The purpose of this sensory profile is to increase your awareness of how sensory encounters affect you.

 Indicate your patterns by placing an X in the appropriate box. (Refer to page 72)

	AVOIDER	BYSTANDER	CRAVER	DETECTOR
Tactile				
Vestibular				
Visual				
Auditory				
Proprioception				
Olfactory				
Gustatory				

THE SCIENCE OF SELF-REFLECTION

It is now time to discover how sensory experiences are impacting your life. This knowledge is priceless. It will help you modify or avoid sensory experiences so you can reduce your stress and increase your self-confidence. This will enable you to be successful in all areas of your life.

The first activity in this session is the *Science of Self-Reflection Assessment*. It will help you recognize how specific situations impact anxiety and how sensory patterns influence your behaviors. This will allow you to implement changes that will reduce your stress.

SELF-REFLECTION ASSESSMENT

 Read the following statements and indicate how often the statement describes you.

HOW OFTEN DOES THIS STATEMENT DESCRIBE YOU?	ALWAYS More than 50% of the time	SOMETIMES Less than 50% of the time	NEVER
1. You feel overwhelmed in crowded places.			
2. You hide or disappear when guests come to visit.			
3. You become upset by unexpected change in plans.			
4. You feel anxious when you are alone.			
5. You feel anxious when you lack control in a situation.			
6. You prefer scheduled activities over free time.			
7. You have difficulty making or keeping friends.			
8. You feel overwhelmed.			
9. You feel like you don't fit in with your peers.			
10. You care for other people more than yourself.			
11. You dislike surprises.			
12. You feel anxious when going to new places.			
13. You have extreme mood swings.			
14. You dislike change, preferring consistency.			
15. You overreact to minor situations.			
16. You act abusively toward self or others.			
17. You have thoughts of inflicting self-harm.			
18. You have panic attacks.			
19. You have strong feelings of anger or rage.			
20. You feel sad or hopeless.			
21. You are plagued by fears and phobias.			
22. You have an outburst if unsuccessful at tasks.			
23. You are stubborn or oppositional.			
24. You feel misunderstood.			
25. You cry more easily than others.			

This assessment is designed to help you recognize stressors in your life. Learning to identify situations that trigger your stress is the first step in managing them. Stress does not only affect your emotional well-being; it will also impact your self-esteem and social engagement.

Life-Changing Moment...

AN INTERESTING SENSORY PREFERENCE

I have three children who were each born 13 months apart. I can vividly remember a day back when they were 1, 2, and three-years-old. I had to take all three of them grocery shopping with me. I was exhausted before leaving the house, worried that one would cry, wander off, or would suddenly need to use the bathroom.

I wondered if we would cause a scene that invited sneers, or if my children would bring a smile to passersby. I had witnessed both and knew how hard this task could be with young children. Grocery shopping can be stressful for parents who bring their toddlers, but it can also be stressful for children. The grocery store exposes shoppers to many sensory encounters: the sweet smells of the bakery, the potent odors from the seafood department, and the extreme temperature change from one department to the next. There are also lots of people, sounds, and things to see. Undeniably, there is a lot of sensory information to process.

This particular day, two of my three little ones were especially difficult. Nothing I did seemed to calm them. I could not finish shopping fast enough. Their cries invited the sneers and the looks of disapproval that this tired mother dreaded. As we neared the last aisle of the store, one child was crying and clinging to my legs, another was in my arms wailing, and the baby was sitting in the front of the cart, smiling ear to ear. I tried playful re-direction to calm them down, but it did not help. I finally gave in to the pressure and raised my voice, instructing them to 'quiet down' At that moment, an older gentleman suddenly grabbed my arm. I prepared myself to be reprimanded, but instead, his insightful words made me weak in the knees.

The man told me I should not quiet the children. He said that their sounds were beautiful, music to his ears. I was confused. He went on to explain that he was a survivor of the Holocaust. He said that he did not hear a child's voice or a baby's cry for a very long time because the war had claimed the lives of so many children. With tears in his eyes, he said, "The sound of a child means there is the hope of a future generation. It is the hope that life will go on." With that, he smiled and stroked my teary children's faces. I was taken aback, overwhelmed by words.

I have never felt the same about the sound of children, whether they are laughing or crying. I will always remember his insightful words and cherish every sound that a child makes because these sounds represent the hope of a new generation.

Sensory Preferences

Very often, our sensory preferences fade into the background of our hectic days. We experience amazing sensory events on the subconscious level, yet their value in making life enjoyable is often overlooked. When we bring these events to a conscious level, we appreciate their magnificence and the powerful influence they have on our lives.

It is not surprising that we each have our own unique sensory preferences. For example, some people like to watch and listen to the water cascading over rocks as it rushes down the stream. Others enjoy watching hawks circling in the expansive sky or the sound of dried leaves crunching beneath their feet.

It is not only the experiences of nature that make our lives complete. The colorful lights from the city, the smell of coffee roasting, or listening to music can also be fulfilling. One client shared that he enjoyed touching the bait while fishing,

while another said that she liked feeling her snake as it slithered over her body. It is easy to see how a particular sensory encounter can be enjoyable for some people but disliked by others.

When considering sensory likes and dislikes, the context and coding of the encounter must be considered. For example, the snow is quickly falling this evening here in New Jersey. Over a foot of snow is covering the ground and adorning trees. It is a beauty that no artist could replicate; however, this same snow might become a stressful sensory event when driving to work in the morning. This illustrates how a sensory event can produce feel-good chemicals at one time and stress-producing chemicals at another.

Sensory likes and dislikes can be multi-dimensional and ever-changing. The secret to using sensory strategies to reduce stress is to recognize how a sensory encounter affects us. These insights will teach us how to manage sensory experiences so we can increase happiness and reduce stress.

SENSORY PREFERENCE ASSESSMENT

 For this therapeutic activity, you will identify five (5) sensory encounters that you enjoy and determine how they make you feel. Record your answers below.

SENSES	LIST FIVE ENCOUNTERS YOU LIKE AND HOW EACH ONE MAKES YOU FEEL (CALM, ENERGIZED, OR BOTH)
Things you like to see	
Things you like to hear	
Things you like to touch	
Things you like to taste	
Things you like to smell	
Movement-related activities you enjoy	

Life-Changing Moment...

MY ACHILLES' HEEL

One morning, a woman sat in the chair next to me at church. She quietly sat in her seat as the congregation sang songs of praise. When the music stopped, the pastor stood to speak. At the same time, the woman reached into her bag and pulled out a box of crackers. The noises from the wrapper and her chewing were not only annoying, it also made it hard to hear the sermon.

She continued to smack her lips as she crunched on each cracker. I tried to ignore her, but the sound was irritating. I could feel my stress level rising because mouth noises are my Achilles' heel. Typically, not much bothers me. I am known for being very patient and easygoing; however, these sounds were having a disturbing effect on me.

The chewing sounds ignited a sense of rage that is hard to describe. I could feel the stress building inside of me each time this woman bit into another cracker. I was surprised by how much this situation impacted me. I started to imagine that I was transforming into another creature, like in an old werewolf movie, because inwardly, I was changing. I arrived at church happy and calm, but now I was feeling frustrated and confrontational. I realized I had to move away before I said something that I might later regret, so I moved to the back of the church for the rest of the service.

Surprisingly, the feeling of frustration and stress lingered long after the service. This made me wonder how sensory experiences might be the under-lying reason we dislike a person or a place. For instance, if it had been my first time at church, I might have left thinking that I do not like church because I found the experience stressful. Thankfully, I recognized that it was not the church service that I disliked; it was the offensive sensory encounter. Yet, it is easy to see how someone might confuse the two.

Therefore, it is important to identify the reasons why we do not like some-one or something. It may not be sounds that bother us; it could be odors or touch experiences that cause us to dislike something or someone. The more we learn about our sensory likes and dislikes, the easier it will be for us to deci-pher what sensory encounters are affecting our perception of people or places.

SENSORY CHALLENGE ASSESSMENT

You recently identified sensory experiences that increase the feel-good chemicals in your brain. For this activity, you need to identify three (3) encounters for each sense that make you feel anxious or uncomfortable. Having learned about the senses, you should have a better understanding as to why these situations make you feel this way.

Three things you do not like to see	
Three things you do not like to hear	
Three things you do not like to touch	
Three things you do not like to taste	
Three things you do not like to smell	
Three movement-related activities that you do not enjoy	

SENSATIONAL ENVIRONMENTS

The therapeutic activities in this session will teach you how to evaluate sensory experiences in your environments. This will help you identify the sensory encounters that increase your anxiety so that you can limit or avoid the offense source. You will also evaluate your sleep environment to determine how sensory events are impacting your sleep.

SESSION GOALS:

☐ Complete the *Environmental Analysis* to identify sensory encounters that contribute to your stress. This will enable you to make modifications that will reduce your stress.

☐ Review the Science of a Good Night's Sleep and evaluate sensory encounters that might be impacting your sleep performance.

☐ Complete the *Sleep Routine Checklist* and *Sleep Study Log* to monitor your sleep performance and identify situations that disrupt your sleep.

Please visit **http://www.SensoryAuthority.com/reader-bonus** to download additional copies of the therapeutic exercises contained in this book.

Life-Changing Moment...

I THOUGHT YOU LOVED IT THERE

One winter evening, my husband and I went out to dinner. He took me to a unique log cabin restaurant that boasted cathedral ceilings, a massive stone fireplace, and was decorated in my favorite rustic décor. The food was delicious, and I knew this would now become a favorite eatery.

Months later, we dined there again. The staff was friendly and engaging, the service was excellent, and the food was once again outstanding. However, the next time my husband asked me to go back to that restaurant for dinner, I suggested we go somewhere else. Confused, he said, "I thought you loved it there." He was right; I did love it there, so why didn't I want to go back? It was perplexing, even for me. I then remembered it was chilly the last time we went, so I grabbed a sweater and agreed to go.

As we sat by the beautiful fireplace enjoying our food, I started feeling anxious. It was then that I realized why I had suggested we go somewhere else. Although the restaurant was not loud, the cathedral ceiling allowed sounds in the room to echo. I heard forks tapping against plates, spoons stirring coffee, and people eating their food. These are the very noises that are known to increase my stress.

Months later, when we were invited by friends to eat at that restaurant, I brought my sweater and asked to be seated in a booth along the wall, knowing it would help filter the irritating noises. These simple modifications changed my dining experience. This time, it was pleasurable and stress-free.

Analyzing Your Environments

Have you ever turned down an invitation without readily knowing the reason why you declined? For example, let us suppose that you and your family are invited to go on a five-day ski trip to Vermont with three other families. Your family is excited, but you refuse the offer. Maybe you refused because you do not like skiing or wearing the heavy, bulky clothing that is needed in the cold months of winter. It is also possible that you do not enjoy long car rides or that you would feel cramped traveling with all the equipment and people.

Maybe you do not enjoy being with such a large group of people or adjusting your schedule to accommodate theirs during a trip? It might also be that you need quiet time to feel composed, which would be hard to get with such a large crowd. Perhaps you declined because the trip was too long. You could have tolerated the crowd for two days, but not for five. A trip like this also requires a lot of gear, which means clutter and disorganization, so you decided not to go. This upsets your family, who liked the idea of going on this trip. This friendly invitation has now caused you more stress than joy. Therefore, it is important to evaluate circumstances to identify the stressors.

People do not always know the exact reason why they refuse an invitation. They only know that something makes them feel uneasy. If they learned how to identify what is causing their dismay, they might find that advocating to make a few minor changes would allow them to enjoy the event. For example, if someone refused this invite because of noise or lack of personal space, they could drive in a separate vehicle or stay in a private room. If it were the disruption of their routine, they could establish their own itinerary, scheduling time to include others. If the length of the trip were the problem, perhaps they could go for a shorter time.

This example illustrates how analyzing a situation to identify stressors can help reduce a person's anxiety. Most people lump together the totality of an event, failing to recognize that individual sensory encounters contribute to the overall experience. When challenging encounters are identified, people should advocate for modifications to accommodate their needs.

The next activity is designed to help you identify stressors in various environments. It provides an excellent foundation for determining what causes you to feel anxious. This awareness will enable you to reduce stress by modifying your environment.

Science of Sensory Environments

The next therapeutic activity teaches you how to identify stressors in your environment, so you modify those situations to make them more pleasurable. Seemingly minor stressors are often contributors to chronic stress. Things like a closet door left open, a room full of clutter, or the sound of a squeaky door can produce cortisol, affecting your emotional stability.

As you complete the *Environmental Analysis*, you will identify the everyday occurrences contributing to your stress so you can make simple adjustments to accommodate your sensory needs. The following is an example of environmental analysis:

In the family room, I would like to change the following:

- ***Sensory Stressor:*** The glare from the window that obscures the TV.

- *Solution:* Install blinds or rearrange the furniture.

- *Sensory Stressor:* The odor from the litter box.

- *Solution:* Relocate the litter box or use pet-friendly air fresheners.

- *Sensory Stressor:* Noise from the adjoining room.

- *Solution:* Install doors between rooms or rearrange furniture to reduce noise.

Below are some points to consider when analyzing an environment to identify stressors:

Sights: Are the lights too bright, too dim, or is there a glare? Is the décor too busy? Is there too much clutter to look at, or is the room too bare? Are the colors too bright or too dark? Are there moving objects that are distracting?

Sounds: Can you hear people talking, music playing, or bothersome repetitive noises that interrupt what you are doing? Is there noise from traffic, pets, or appliances, or is the environment too quiet?

Smells: Are there offensive odors in your environment like garbage, cigarettes, foods, pet odors, or outdoor smells? Is the scent of cleaning products, perfumes, or air fresheners bothersome?

Taste: Consider if food is too bland, spicy, chewy, or crunchy? Is it excessively mushy, stale, or dry? Is the temperature of food too hot or too cold?

Touch: Is space limited, causing people or things to bump into you, or is it too big and open? Is furniture too hard or soft? Are surfaces too rough or smooth? Are there unpleasant textures like sticky, wet, or greasy that affect your experience?

Movement: Is movement restricted or limited in the environment? Are there obstacles or too many people or things restricting your space? Are there too many steps or uneven surfaces?

POINT TO PONDER...

It is important to evaluate all aspects of an environment, including both sensory and logistics. For example, if you are petite like me, and other people placed commonly used items on the highest shelf in the cabinet, this inconvenience would cause stress. This stress is easily eliminated by communicating your needs to others and modifying the environment. This is why it is crucial to learn how to identify stressors, so you can make adjustments to rectify the problem.

ENVIRONMENTAL ANALYSIS

How many different environments do you encounter in a day? You likely work in one setting, eat meals in another, and relax in yet another. Throughout the day, you are exposed to stressors in different environments. Once you identify the situations that are increasing your stress, you can make modifications to reduce them.

Complete the chart below to identify the sensory experiences in your environment that increase stress. Be sure to consider all the possible encounters associated with each sense.

ANALYZE SENSORY ENCOUNTERS IN THE FOLLOWING ENVIRONMENTS	SIGHTS	SOUNDS	SMELLS	TOUCH
TV Room				
Computer Room				
Dining Area				
Bedroom				
Bathroom				
Office				
Car				

THE SCIENCE OF A GOOD NIGHT'S SLEEP

People should spend approximately one-third of their life sleeping, yet over 40% of Americans report they are not getting enough sleep. Studies indicate that disrupted sleep patterns contribute to behavioral problems, inattentiveness, and problems with learning. It increases the risk of heart failure, stroke, obesity, diabetes, and hypertension. Drowsiness from poor sleep is responsible for approximately 20% of car accidents, and it is the number one cause of workplace accidents. Interestingly, trouble sleeping is second to pain on the list of complaints made by patients.

15 FACTS YOU SHOULD KNOW ABOUT SLEEP
Deep sleep helps to prune the brain, preparing it for learning new things.
Sleep helps with longevity.
Sleep helps you to look younger by ensuring a healthy turnover of cells.
Sleep strengthens your immune system.
Sleep improves your concentration, memory, and cognitive function.
Sleep improves relationships, it decreases arguments and increases empathy.
Sleep reduces stress headaches.
Sleep reduces the risk of depression.
Sleep reduces the occurrence of mood disorders.
Sleep is a pain reliever. It increases your pain tolerance.
Sleep reduces inflammation in the body, reducing your risk for cancer, diabetes, and heart conditions.
Sleep deprivation reduces muscle strength and power.
Less than 5 hours of sleep per night quadruples your risk for a car accident.
Sleep helps with weight management. Poor sleep makes you more prone to stress, reduces your energy, and increases your appetite contributing to unwanted pounds.
Less than six hours of sleep a night can reduce your sex drive.

There is no question that a good night's sleep contributes to reducing stress and anxiety, but how do we get a good night's sleep?

Life-Changing Moment...

FOUNTAIN OF YOUTH

In college, the professor gave our class an assignment to monitor our sleep performance for two weeks. She provided strategies that would help us achieve a good night's sleep. The students complained, stating that they did not have time to sleep because of their studies, but the professor was undeterred. She said the assignment was doable.

After the first week of monitoring sleep, the students reported that the modifications the professor suggested helped them to sleep longer. Interestingly, everyone looked healthier and more vibrant. One student, in particular, looked years younger. Everyone was impressed by how sleep affected this man. It was truly remarkable.

The second week's results were utterly amazing: most students had better posture and engaged more socially. They were also more confident and less anxious. All students reported that they felt more alert, and everyone looked younger, especially the one student who had significant improvement after the first week. His transformation was extraordinary. It was as if he had discovered the fountain of youth.

He did not only look younger; he moved about like a younger man. He had a youthful bounce in his step that could not be ignored, and everyone noticed that he smiled and interacted more with his peers. It was evident that sleep enabled him to function at his best.

He was also surprised by the impact sleep had on his life. He said he never felt better and learning to get a goodnight's sleep significantly changed every aspect of his life. Today, now a professor himself, he gives his students that same assignment, knowing it will be life changing.

The Secret to Getting A Good Night's Sleep

Society does not value time spent sleeping, as sleep is often associated with laziness. In addition to social pressure, other factors affect sleep performance, including stress, energy-boosting products, and exposure to screen time. Inadequate sleep impacts our mental health. It affects our mood, judgment, anxiety, and depression. It also affects our motivation, weight, and immune system. A lack of sleep also intensifies unhealthy behaviors such as smoking, over-eating, and excessive drinking.

The following recommendations have been found to improve sleep.

Establish A Pre-Sleep Routine

It is important to establish a relaxing 15-30 minute pre-sleep ritual. This could include the following:

- Read a book, take a warm bath, soak your feet in warm water, rock in a rocking chair, use self-massage techniques, or have someone provide deep pressure or light touch massage.

- Enjoy a light snack. Eat foods that can help promote sleep: Milk contains tryptophan, which is a sleep-promoting substance. Other foods that may improve sleep include tuna, halibut, pumpkin, artichokes, avocados, almonds, eggs, peaches, walnuts, apricots, oats, asparagus, potatoes, buckwheat, and bananas.

- Avoid strenuous exercise and bright artificial light, such as from a TV or computer screen, one hour before bedtime. The light suppresses the production of melatonin, which affects your circadian rhythm.

- Reduce anxiety before going to bed by using relaxation techniques.

- Avoid stressful or stimulating activities such as doing work or discussing emotional issues. The stress hormone, cortisol, arouses the nervous system. It increases attention and energy, which disrupts sleep.

- Try writing down your problems. If you can think of a solution, check it off. If you cannot think of one at this time, add it to the list of concerns to be dealt with in the morning. This will help you relax because this system becomes part of your solution, which alleviates stress.

- Practice mindfulness, deep breathing, guided imagery, and progressive muscle relaxation (relaxing one muscle at a time).

Develop A Sleep Schedule

- Establish a routine sleep schedule: Go to bed around the same time each night and wake up at approximately the same time each morning.

Tips for Relaxing Before Bedtime

Did you know that worrying stimulates the body to produce the adrenaline, which will keep you awake? There are several options for relaxing at bedtime.

- Breathe slowly. Imagine ocean waves rising and breaking.

- Mentally take yourself to a quiet, restful, relaxing place in your mind.

- Do not obsess about falling asleep. Focus on rest.

- Do not Be a Nighttime Clock-Watcher: Staring at the clock in your bedroom can increase stress, making it harder to fall asleep. Turn your clock's face away from you.

Make the Bedroom A Sleep Only Zone

- The bedroom should only be used for sleeping. Remove TVs, computers, and cell phones from this room.

- Parents: Do not use the bedroom as a time-out room. The child will learn to associate this room with heightened feelings of anxiety. This room should be a sanctuary for rest.

Sensory Strategies for A Good Night's Sleep

Evaluate Your Sleep Environment

- Keep the bedroom quiet, cool, and dark at night.

Tactile: The Sense of Touch

- Evaluate the comfort of your bed, pillows, sheets, blankets, and sleepwear.

- Consider using flannel sheets for a soft touch and temperature control.

- Consider using a weighted blanket for deep pressure touch.

- Try placing a vibrating pillow or handheld massager under the mattress, which creates diffused vibration. This touch sensation tends to be calming to most people. If you find this is soothing, you can purchase a vibrating mattress pad to help you sleep.

- Limit pets in the bedroom if they interrupt sleep.

Visual: The Sense of Sight

- Any amount of light can suppress melatonin production. This makes it hard to fall asleep. Light keeps the nervous system aroused, and melatonin helps to calm it so you can sleep.

- An hour before bedtime, dim the lights and turn off the TV and computer, then make your bedroom as dark as possible using blackout shades if necessary. Toss a scarf over the alarm clock to increase the darkness.

- Declutter room. Clutter is visually stimulating.

Olfactory: *The Sense of Smell*

- Try different aromatherapies or scented items for environmental support.

- Sniff the sheets and blankets: If you are sensory seeking and enjoy a light scent, wash them in scented detergents. If you are sensory-avoiding and need them to be scent-free, wash them in unscented detergent.

Auditory: *The Sense of Hearing*

- Reduce extraneous noise by using earplugs or a white noise machine.

- Listen to soft, quiet music as part of your pre-sleep routine or early sleep routine.

- Avoid loud, stimulating, alerting music for at least 30 minutes before your bedtime.

- Wearing noise-canceling headphones or earplugs at night can be helpful.

- Listening to an inspiring story at a low volume may help distract from stressful thoughts.

What to Avoid To Get A Good Night's Sleep

Caffeine and Nicotine

- Avoid nicotine (for example, cigarettes) and caffeine (including caffeinated soda, coffee, pain relievers, tea, and chocolate) because they are stimulants that interfere with sleep.

- The effects of caffeine can last as long as 8 hours, so having coffee in the late afternoon can make it hard for you to fall asleep at night.

Spicy Foods

- Spicy and highly acidic foods are common causes of heartburn, which can interfere with your sleep: consume milder meals before bedtime.

Alcohol

- Alcohol affects your sleep patterns. It may make you sleepy initially, but it arouses the brain 4—5 hours later, causing you to wake up. This hyper-aroused state can persist for several hours.

Important Considerations for A Good Night's Sleep

Schedule Daily Physical Activity

- You must exert energy to become physically tired.

- Schedule 30 minutes of aerobic activity into your daytime routine. Studies show 30 minutes of exercise improves sleep, almost as well as sleeping pills.

Supplements

- Taking a melatonin supplement in the evening may help you fall asleep faster, but you should always consult with your physician before taking any supplements.

Sensory Tools and Strategies

- Perform joint compression and joint traction activities before bedtime. Deep pressure applied to arms and legs, also called hand hugs or squeezes, can help people relax.

- Try applying magnesium oil to the bottom of feet at bedtime or taking the supplement.

Check with your doctor before taking any supplements.

- Try a weighted blanket or heavy quilt for deep pressure input, which is calming for some people.

- Drink a warm, decaffeinated drink before bed.

- Wear socks to bed. Cold extremities impact sleep.

- Use a soft make-up brush or fabrics to apply a self-soothing light touch on the body.

Technology

- There are several apps available today to help people relax and sleep. I encourage you to explore the available options.

SLEEP ROUTINE CHECKLIST

DID YOU...	SLEEP ROUTINE
	Make the bedroom a sleep only zone. (No TV or technology)
	Perform a pre-sleep routine 15 to 30 minutes before bed
	Establish a sleep schedule
	Use anxiety-reducing strategies before bed
	Evaluate sensory factors in bedroom: Sight, sounds, smell, textures, & temperature
	Avoid caffeine, spicy foods, alcohol, and screen time
	Incorporate 30 minutes of exercise into your daytime routine

SLEEP STUDY LOG

 Complete the sleep study log to evaluate your sleep performance.

SLEEP PATTERNS	SUN	MON	TUES	WED	THURS	FRI	SAT
Date							
Time you entered bed							
Approximate the time you fell asleep							
Number of times your sleep was disturbed							
Cause of disturbance							
Time you woke-up							
Time you got out of bed							

How did you feel at the end of the first week? _____

What can you do to reduce the situations that interrupted your sleep?

_____

_____

_____

YOUR SENSATIONAL LIFE

In this session, you will learn how your sensory profile influences your interests in hobbies. Investing time in pursuing interests will not only help you achieve short- and long-term goals; it will introduce you to people with similar interests., which helps establish friendships.

Have you ever wondered how some people achieve their goals and still find time to enjoy their hobbies? Successful people understand the importance of developing a plan to manage their time and resources. The activities in this session will help you identify your interests and create a plan to achieve success.

SESSION GOALS:

☐ Review the Science of Interests and Hobbies to explore how sensory preferences impact your interests. Discover how shared interests serve as a foundation for establishing relationships.

☐ Complete the *Interests and Hobbies* checklist. Consider how your sensory profile impacts your choices.

☐ Review the Science of Goal Achievement and complete the *Goal Analysis* to identify and prioritize your goals.

☐ Complete *Your Goal Planner* to learn the strategies that lead to success.

Please visit **http://www.SensoryAuthority.com/reader-bonus** to download additional copies of the therapeutic exercises contained in this book.

Life-Changing Moment...

WHAT GOOD IS A TOOL IF YOU DON'T USE IT?

Over the years, I have been perplexed by the fact that people seek therapy services, yet they seem to overlook the importance of implementing the therapeutic strategies suggested to them. I understand people are busy, but what good is a tool if you do not use it?

Recently, this happened with one young man I was treating. His family sought services because he refused to go to school and was having trouble making friends. Upon meeting him, I found that he was extremely friendly and smart, but he lacked confidence and struggled with anxiety, which affected his ability to succeed.

Over the course of a few weeks, I created a sensory diet for him. I also had him complete the Interest and Hobbies Checklist and gave his parents a list of hobbies that interested him. I explained how pursuing his hobbies would boost his self-esteem and introduce him to other children who had similar interests. This would open the door for him to form friendships and build his self-confidence.

Week after week, his parents would bring him to therapy, explaining how they did not have time to implement the strategies. I understood their time constraints, but I knew these strategies were a significant part of the solution to his problems.

Months later, I received a heartfelt message from this boy's mother. She contacted me because we had not seen each other for some time due to the Covid-19 pandemic. She said that she could not wait to tell me how great her son was doing. She shared how she implemented the sensory diet and helped her son pursue some of his interests. Excitedly, she reported that her son was now excelling in school. His confidence had improved, and he made some friends. She ended the call, saying, "You know, Ms. Judi, I only wish we had tried this months ago."

Although success stories like his warm my heart, I cannot help but feel a little sad that it often takes so long for clients to use the therapeutic tools provided to them. I hope this story encourages you to implement the strategies learned in this program as I am confident you will find they are life changing.

The Science of Interest & Hobbies

Hobbies bring meaning and purpose to our lives and they introduce us to people who share the similar interests. This fosters social engagement to develop friendships and a sense of community. Social connections have been shown to reduce stress and depression, help fight disease, and decrease the risk of dementia. Friendships also slow the aging process, sharpen our cognitive skills, and prolong our life.

Hobbies create opportunities for us to achieve success in the activities that we enjoy while activating feel-good chemicals in our brains. Successful participation has a positive impact on our brain chemistry. The more we do something, the better we get at it. This inspires us to continue participating in this activity, which nurtures our sense of achievement.

The next activity is designed to help you identify hobbies that interest you. It will also indicate how sensory likes and dislikes affect those interests while revealing if you prefer indoor or outdoor activities and individual or group activities. Pursuing these hobbies will increase your self-esteem and social circle while reducing your stress.

INTEREST AND HOBBIES CHECKLIST

 Place a check next to the hobbies that interest you.

Activities Involving Water

- ☐ Swimming
- ☐ Jet Skiing
- ☐ Snorkeling
- ☐ Canoeing
- ☐ Paddle Boarding
- ☐ Skim Boarding
- ☐ Rowing
- ☐ Sunbathing
- ☐ Fishing
- ☐ Water Skiing
- ☐ Surfing
- ☐ Kayaking
- ☐ Parasailing
- ☐ Body Boarding
- ☐ Water Parks
- ☐ Crabbing or Clamming
- ☐ Boating
- ☐ Scuba Diving
- ☐ Tubing
- ☐ White Water Rafting
- ☐ Diving
- ☐ Wind Surfing
- ☐ Aqua Jogging
- ☐ Walk on the Beach

Activities Involving Snow and Ice

- [ ] Sledding
- [ ] Ice Skating
- [ ] Snow Boarding
- [ ] Down Hill Skiing
- [ ] Ice Fishing
- [ ] Tubing
- [ ] Cross Country Skiing
- [ ] Snowmobiling
- [ ] Ice Climbing

Competitive Group Activities

- [ ] Football
- [ ] Lacrosse
- [ ] Field Hockey
- [ ] Basketball
- [ ] Baseball
- [ ] Soccer
- [ ] Ice Hockey
- [ ] Racquetball
- [ ] Volleyball
- [ ] Soft Ball
- [ ] Roller Hockey
- [ ] Cheerleading

Small Group or Individual Outdoor Activities

- [ ] Hunting
- [ ] Tennis
- [ ] Paintball
- [ ] Jogging
- [ ] Bike Riding
- [ ] Rollerblading
- [ ] Badminton
- [ ] Four Wheeling
- [ ] Sightseeing
- [ ] Nascar Races
- [ ] Flying Lessons
- [ ] Whale Watching
- [ ] Kite Flying
- [ ] RV Traveling
- [ ] Amusement Parks
- [ ] Trains
- [ ] Mini-Golf
- [ ] Vehicle Restoration
- [ ] Storm Chaser
- [ ] Camping
- [ ] Track and Field
- [ ] Running
- [ ] Golf
- [ ] Dirt bike Riding
- [ ] Horseback Riding
- [ ] Trampoline
- [ ] Nature Walks
- [ ] Airshows
- [ ] Lighthouses
- [ ] Classic Cars
- [ ] Go-Karts
- [ ] Astronomy
- [ ] Gardening
- [ ] Historical Landmarks
- [ ] Cruises
- [ ] National Parks
- [ ] People Watching
- [ ] Garage Sales
- [ ] Hiking
- [ ] Airsoft
- [ ] Walking
- [ ] Skeet Shooting
- [ ] Skateboarding
- [ ] Horseshoes/Bocce
- [ ] Tetherball
- [ ] Picnics
- [ ] Festivals
- [ ] Battleships
- [ ] Caverns/Mines
- [ ] Bird Watching
- [ ] Star Gazing
- [ ] Visiting Zoo
- [ ] BBQ's/Parties
- [ ] Travel
- [ ] Driving
- [ ] Work on Cars/Motors
- [ ] Drones

Extreme Outdoor Adventures

- ☐ Bungee Jumping
- ☐ Sky Diving
- ☐ Hot Air Balloons
- ☐ Helicopter Rides

- ☐ Gliding
- ☐ Mountain Climbing
- ☐ Flying
- ☐ Base Jumping

- ☐ Zip Lines
- ☐ Rock Climbing
- ☐ Hang Gliding
- ☐ Jet Pack

Small Group or Individual Indoor Activities

- ☐ Exercising
- ☐ Fencing
- ☐ Arcades
- ☐ Body Building
- ☐ Hatchet Throwing
- ☐ Wrestling
- ☐ Yoga
- ☐ Aquarium
- ☐ Planetarium
- ☐ Botanical Gardens
- ☐ Take a Class
- ☐ Comedy
- ☐ Watch a Movie with Friends
- ☐ Home Remodeling
- ☐ Live Entertainment
- ☐ Chess
- ☐ Ham Radio
- ☐ Learn New Language
- ☐ Advocacy
- ☐ Visit with Relatives
- ☐ Scouts
- ☐ Museums
- ☐ Fashion
- ☐ Photography
- ☐ Attend Lectures
- ☐ Teaching
- ☐ Book Club

- ☐ Gymnastics
- ☐ Bowling
- ☐ Table Tennis
- ☐ Karate
- ☐ Shooting Range
- ☐ Roller Rinks
- ☐ Zumba
- ☐ Wine Making
- ☐ Space Center
- ☐ Antiquing
- ☐ Take a Tour
- ☐ Magic
- ☐ Impersonations
- ☐ Make a Video
- ☐ Sporting Events
- ☐ Flower Arranging
- ☐ Fantasy Sports
- ☐ Business Ventures
- ☐ Operas
- ☐ Animals
- ☐ Church Activities
- ☐ Shopping
- ☐ Make-up Artistry
- ☐ Cleaning
- ☐ Library
- ☐ Garage Sales
- ☐ Fundraising

- ☐ Dancing
- ☐ Billiards
- ☐ Boxing
- ☐ Kickboxing
- ☐ MMA
- ☐ Woodworking
- ☐ Pilates
- ☐ Craft Shows
- ☐ Science Center
- ☐ Sightseeing
- ☐ Acting
- ☐ Darts
- ☐ Storm Chaser
- ☐ Science Activities
- ☐ Gambling
- ☐ DJ
- ☐ Acrobatics
- ☐ Product Design
- ☐ Volunteering
- ☐ Farming
- ☐ Dining Out
- ☐ Interior Decorating
- ☐ Hairstyling
- ☐ Organizing
- ☐ Politics
- ☐ Tutoring
- ☐ Collectibles

Individual Activities

☐ Card Games	☐ Board Games	☐ Video Games
☐ Crossword Puzzles	☐ Painting	☐ Drawing
☐ Cooking	☐ Baking	☐ Cake Decorating
☐ Knitting/Crocheting	☐ Reading	☐ Writing
☐ Sewing	☐ Ceramics	☐ Leather Crafts
☐ Metal Art	☐ Crafts	☐ Movies
☐ Jewelry Making	☐ Trivia	☐ Singing
☐ Play an Instrument	☐ Whittling	☐ Sculpting
☐ Watch TV or You Tube	☐ Computer Games	☐ Collecting
☐ Puzzles	☐ Social Media	☐ Graphic Design
☐ Journaling	☐ Meditation	☐ Research
☐ Model Building	☐ Listening to Music	☐ Brain Games
☐ Candle Making	☐ 3D Printing	☐ Couponing
☐ Juggling	☐ Quilting	☐ Origami
☐ Sand Art	☐ Scrapbooking	☐ Blogging
☐ Astrology	☐ Taxidermy	☐ Investing
☐ Film Making	☐ Unique Crafting	☐ Animation
☐ Song Writing	☐ Robotics	☐ Airbrushing
☐ Coffee Roasting	☐ Coloring	☐ Radio Controlled
☐ Health Studies	☐ Nutrition Studies	☐ Designing/Creating
☐ Web Site Design	☐ Video Game Design	☐ Composing

Other hobbies not listed:

_____

_____

_____

_____

Life-Changing Moment...

CLIMB AND MAINTAIN

I do not often have time to watch TV, but I try to watch Joel Osteen, Joyce Meyer, or Steven Furtick at some point during my day. Their inspirational messages fortify my soul and help direct my path. One evening, I happened to see a guest speaker who was speaking at Joel Osteen's church. I had never seen him before, but he was likable, and his message was life changing.

He said his name was Tyler Perry, and that he had gone to school to become a minister but soon realized God had a different plan. He explained that he was now a writer and producer, which meant he had to travel often. He said that flying made him nervous; and although he had tried traveling by other means, ground travel was not time-efficient, so he had to overcome his fear of flying.

One day, he saw a man flying a model plane at the park. This gave him an idea: if he could understand how a plane works, it might alleviate his fears. He purchased a model plane; but when he tried to operate it, it crashed to the ground. He bought a second one and crashed that one, too. When he returned to buy his third model plane, the store owner asked if he would like a lesson on how to fly the plane. Mr. Perry accepted his offer. After the tutorial, Mr. Perry was able to fly his model plane successfully. This inspired him to take flying lessons.

When he mastered his skills and earned his pilot's license, he looked into buying a plane. He conducted extensive research and found one that had numerous safety features, so he arranged a test flight. The first flight was smooth and steady, so he decided to buy the plane. However, on the day, he was to finalize the deal, something told him to take the plane for one more test flight.

Later that day, he and the salesman took the plane for a short trip. The flight was smooth until they hit turbulence. The aircraft shook vigorously. Mr. Perry pleaded with the pilot to land the plane and get him back down to the ground. The pilot notified air traffic control, but a calm voice instructed them to 'fly high and maintain.' The pilot took the plane higher, and the flight was smooth. They flew above the turbulence until they reached their destination.

Mr. Perry used this story to illustrate that when life gets hard, it is normal for us to want to give up and go back to where we started. However, if we have faith, we can rise above the difficulties and continue our journey by trusting God.

The Science of Goal Achievement

Today people are used to instant gratification and perfection. Gone are the days when people meticulously turned the dial, hoping to hear a song through the static on their transistor radios. These days, people expect immediate results with no room for errors; however, there a price to be paid for this progress.

People are no longer tolerant of imperfections in themselves or others. In this world of auto-tune, spellcheck, and Photoshop, the nuances of flaws have been erased; and manufactured perfections remain. This leads to unrealistic expectations and anxiety. We have also learned impatience, which affects our ability to plan long-term goals.

Goal Planning

Goals establish meaning and purpose in our life. They motivate us and structure our steps. Much like a finish line defines the end of a race, goal achievement needs to be clearly defined. Success stimulates the reward center in the brain. This increases our self-worth and the motivation to work toward other goals.

People need to have specific short and long-term goals. This helps them to be productive with their time and resources. Goal planning is vital to achieving success. Unlike fantasizing about goal achievement, goal planning outlines the necessary resources and skills, and it organizes the steps to achieve success. Planning also identifies obstacles so you can develop solutions, and it defines the exact point of achievement.

Failures Have a Purpose

Failures are like sandpaper; they rub us the wrong way. They go against our grain and make us feel uncomfortable. Yet, like sandpaper, failures have a purpose. They remove flaws by teaching us and refining our skills.

Failures are inevitable. They are a part of every person's life, but what does it mean to fail? It simply means that we did not achieve our intended goal, but it does not mean that we never will. Failures are disappointing, but they are also our best teachers if we learn from them.

R. H. Macy failed seven times before his department store concept became successful. If you consider how difficult each of these failures must have been for him, you realize one of his greatest assets was learning from them. He had to handle his own sense of discouragement, tainted reputation as an entrepreneur, and financial loss. He had to contend with comments from family and friends. However, Macy turned each failure into a time of reflection, learning from his mistakes, and trying again.

Macy knew something invaluable: failure is not an ending. He understood that these experiences would teach him what he needed to know so that he could be successful one day.

How to Manage Disappointments

Setbacks and disappointments happen to everyone. We all suffer times when we feel worthless or incapable because we have been rejected or failed to achieve success. So how is one to cope with these life-altering disappointments?

There is no definitive formula for managing failures. They leave a person feeling confused, hurt, and embarrassed. However, when you consider the fact that every person experiences failure in their life, you will find that these moments are very often beginnings and not endings. They become the starting point for a new direction.

8 Ways to Manage Disappointments

1. Recognize that everyone has failed at something and that no one is perfect.

2. Failure does not define you. It is not a character flaw.

3. Allow yourself time to experience the pain of defeat while recognizing that you are going to be okay.

4. When things do not work out as planned, see it as a time for personal reflection and growth, enabling you to learn from the experience.

5. Forgive yourself, and those who may have intentionally or unintentionally contributed to this defeat.

6. Failure is merely another life lesson, like falling when learning to walk. You need to get back up and make the necessary adjustments so you can achieve success.

7. If you tried your best, then you did not fail.

8. Always remember: If you fall down 7 times, get up 8.

Identifying and Prioritizing Goals

Goal achievement is possible for everyone. Whether it is a short or long-term goal, goals will require a well-developed plan to realize success. You can identify goals by reflecting on areas of your life to identify things you would like to change. Think about how your life would improve if you achieved these goals. Then you can rate them to determine the ones you will work on first.

The next activity walks you through this process. You will be surprised to see what is revealed when assessing the different areas of your life. Some people discover that calling their family more often is an important goal. Others realize that pursuing their education or spending more time pursuing hobbies is at the top of their list. This insight enables them to develop a plan to achieve their goal.

GOAL ANALYSIS

Reflect on the different areas of daily living and consider your strengths in each area. You will then list things that you would like to improve or change. These are your goals. You will then rate each goal by placing a number 1 next to the goals that would significantly change your life at this time, and a number 2 next to goals that you would like to achieve in the future.

AREAS OF DAILY LIVING	AREAS TO IMPROVE/GOALS	RATING 1 / 2
Example	*Exercise 3-4 times per week*	1
Self-Care		
Physical Activities		
Diet & Nutrition		
Appearance		
Sleep		
Finances		
Work		
Education		
Relationships		
Social Interactions		
Hobbies/Interests		
Spirituality		

CHOOSING A GOAL

Review the list of goals that you identified, highlighting the ones you rated number 1. From that list, determine which one you would like to achieve at this time and complete the Goal Planner for that goal.

When planning your goal, clearly define what you are trying to achieve and establish a system to measure your success (dollars, weight, quantity, etc.). Your goal must be doable, measurable, and realistic. For example, a goal of losing fifty pounds in one week is not realistic, but a goal of losing two pounds in one week is achievable.

DEFINE THE GOAL YOU WOULD LIKE TO WORK ON

_____

_____

_____

GOAL PLANNER

 Complete the planner for your intended goal.

SUCCESS INVENTORY	WHAT YOU NEED TO ACHIEVE THIS GOAL
Required Resources: People, things, space, time, education, and employees	
Required Skills: What skills are needed to achieve this goal?	
Supportive Services: People, professionals, organizations, and investors.	
Obstacles/Solutions List possible barriers and solutions.	
Method of Accountability How will you measure success? Timelines, weight, money, quantity?	

THE STEPS TO SUCCESS

 Identify where to begin and what steps need to follow to achieve your goal.

Step 1: _____

Step 2: _____

Step 3: _____

Step 4: _____

Step 5: _____

Goal Achievement

After you have developed the plan for your goal, you may have to modify it. Most goals will require periodic re-evaluation and adjustments. This should not discourage you. Modifications are often required to achieve success.

SENSORY DIETS

You will now use your sensory knowledge to create your personalized sensory action plan. In this session, you will learn about sensory diets and their role in organizing the sensory encounters that calm you as well as the ones that energize you. This plan will help you implement the sensory strategies that will improve your life.

SESSION GOALS:

☐ Gain an understanding of sensory diets and how they are used to reduce stress and increase alertness.

☐ Identify the sensory encounters that produce feel-good chemicals in your brain. These are the sensory experiences that can be used to reduce stress.

☐ Identify sensory encounters that can be used to arouse or energize a sluggish nervous system

☐ Use your sensory knowledge to create a personalized *Sensory Action Plan*.

Please visit **http://www.SensoryAuthority.com/reader-bonus** to download additional copies of the therapeutic exercises contained in this book.

Life-Changing Moment...

HAPPY STRESSORS ARE STRESSFUL

A mother cheerfully announces that today is her son's birthday as she walks him into the therapy gym. Naturally, everyone wishes him a happy birthday as he walks by, but the little boy frowns and looks away. His mother said that the past week has been incredibly stressful. She said her son had several meltdowns, and the more she tried to 'cheer him up,' the more he acted out. She then cheerfully spoke about the fun activities she planned to celebrate his birthday, hoping he would be excited, but instead, he looked upset. She was confused because she was only trying to make her son happy.

Across town, there is a young woman who is excited about her college graduation tomorrow night. She proudly tries on her new outfit, preparing for the special event. Happily, she runs to the kitchen, where her mother is busy preparing for the party that will follow the memorable event. Beaming with pride, the young woman says, "Look, Mom. What do you think?" Her mother glances over and replies, "What is wrong with you? We do not have time for this nonsense. We have a houseful of people coming to your party tomorrow night" The young woman is devastated. She thought her mother was happy about her graduation.

Down the road, there lives a dedicated father who worked overtime for years to save enough money to take his family to Disney World. Excitedly, he tells the family that he booked the trip, and his family showers him with affection. Then the children run off, gathering items to take on the trip. Everyone was thrilled.

On the morning they were to leave for Disney, the parents rushed to finish packing and get the house in order. The children impatiently ran around, asking, "Hey Daddy, do you think we will see Mickey? How about Minnie? Will she be there? And will we get to see Cinderella's castle?" They were loud and rambunctious. Their busy father shouted, "Stop playing around! We do not have time for these games. Now go help your mother so we can get going!" The children were confused: they thought this trip was supposed to be fun.

Most of us can relate to these types of stories. We have all felt hurt and confused when people did not respond to something as we had anticipated.

Celebrations, trips, successes, and even unique gifts expose us to different sensory encounters. For example, the young boy did not like all the attention generated by his birthday: he had to look at more faces, hear more voices, and endure more touch experiences with every birthday wish. There were also changes in his routine, which was hard for him.

This was also the case for the mother of the graduate and the father who planned the trip. They were each trying to manage several different sensory experiences at once, including those from their inner senses, as they prepared for a special event. These examples demonstrate that the effect of positive stress is quite similar to the impact of negative stress.

What Is A Sensory Diet?

The term 'sensory diet' was coined by the late Dr. Jean Ayres to describe a set of sensory strategies that can be used to balance the nervous system. This means you can implement certain sensory encounters to reduce stress. You can also employ sensory strategies to energize your nervous system. The sensory diet is similar to compiling a list of foods that establishes a nutritional diet, but instead of providing food options, it provides sensory encounter options to maintain a healthy lifestyle.

The Life Changers Sensory Solutions Program expands on this concept by helping you create a personalized Sensory Action Plan (SAP). Like the sensory diet, the sensory action plan indicates the sensory experiences that you can use to reduce stress or energize your nervous system; however, it also includes sensory encounters that you should limit or avoid. You will create your sensory action plan by reflecting on your processing patterns and the sensory preferences you identified in the therapeutic exercises.

It is important to note that a sensory strategy might work one day, but not be as effective on another. Your tolerance to sensory encounters will fluctuate, similar to being more hungry or tired one day than another. Situations like stress, medical conditions, and environmental factors will also affect your sensory tolerance.

Why Create A Sensory Action Plan?

When people are making plans, they often ask, 'What is there to do around here?' or 'Where should we go for dinner?' even though they have lived in the area for the better part of their lives. They cannot easily recall available options, so they rely on helpful reminders. This is why a sensory action plan is beneficial: it clearly delineates the strategies that can calm or energize you.

If you were to ask people what they do to energize themselves, many would say they splash water on their face or drink coffee. They might not realize that there are countless other ways to arouse their nervous system. For instance, they could listen to invigorating music, smell various scents, sip a cold, carbonated drink, or eat sour foods.

If you asked people how they calm themselves when upset, they might indicate that going for a drive or taking a hot shower helps calm them. However, they could also do things like listen to music, savor the fragrance of a scented candle, or sip a hot drink to reduce their stress, if they found these encounters helped soothe them.

Your Personalized Sensory Action Plan

Reflecting on what you now know about your senses and your unique processing patterns, you should be well equipped to make your personalized Sensory Action Plan. The easy to use templates provide a list of suggested sensory strategies that are commonly used, as well as space for you to record the strategies you identified. You are encouraged to reference your *Interest and Hobbies* checklist and *Sensory Preferences/Challenges* worksheets to identify sensory experiences that can be incorporated into your sensory action plan.

Most activities will stimulate more than one sense. For example, chewing sour candy stimulates your sense of taste, touch, smell, and deep pressure; therefore, you will need to decide where to include this strategy. I recommend that you record it under the sense that benefits you the most. For some people, it may be the taste, but for others, it could be that the deep pressure from chewing.

As you compile your list of strategies, it is important to determine how the encounter makes you feel. You can indicate its effect by marking calming, arousing, or that it is an encounter that you should limit or avoid.

The following is an example of how to complete the templates to create your sensory action plan. In this example, the client indicated that the sound of hammering has an arousing effect, but only when limited. Otherwise, it becomes a stressor.

ACTIVITIES FOR AUDITORY STIMULATION	CALMING	AROUSING	LIMIT OR AVOID
Listen to invigorating music		X	
Sound of rain, wind, or waterfall	X		
Meditation tapes or white noise machines	X		
Hammering		X	X
Sound of someone chewing or whistling			X

THE VESTIBULAR SYSTEM

This system detects movement, balance, positional changes, and spatial orientation. Receptors are stimulated by motion, positional changes, and activities that include spinning, swinging, or flipping.

People benefit from stimulating their vestibular system periodically. The benefits of stimulation can last several hours. Standing, stretching, walking, or swiveling side to side in a chair stimulates the receptors. This improves your balance, posture, and ability to concentrate. However, too much stimulation can cause a sensory overload. Signs of a vestibular overload include dizziness, imbalance, fatigue, headache, nausea, and irritability.

 Complete the chart below by indicating if the suggested activity makes you feel calm, energized, or is one that should be limited or avoided to reduce your stress.

SUGGESTED ACTIVITIES FOR VESTIBULAR STIMULATION	CALMING	ENERGIZING	LIMIT OR AVOID
Driving			
Walking/Hiking			
Riding a Bike			
Running			
Dancing			
Exercising			
Rocking or Swiveling in a Chair			
Boating			
Surfing			
Skiing			
Skating			
Amusement Park Rides			

Complete the chart below by listing the sensory events that shape your life. Indicate if they make you feel calm, energized, or if they should be limited or avoided to manage your stress.

ACTIVITIES YOU IDENTIFIED FOR VESTIBULAR STIMULATION	CALMING	ENERGIZING	LIMIT OR AVOID

THE PROPRIOCEPTIVE SYSTEM (DEEP PRESSURE)

This system detects body awareness, muscle strength, balance, and movement. Heavy lifting, pushing, pulling, and deep pressure stimulates these receptors.

Deep pressure input is calming and organizing. Stimulating these receptors improves body awareness, coordination of movement, posture, and muscle strength. The many benefits of proprioceptive (deep pressure) input can last several hours.

People benefit from wearing compression clothing, weighted hats, neck wraps, or lap pillows that provide continual deep pressure. However, some people prefer intermittent deep pressure from running, jumping, lifting, or pushing.

 Complete the chart below by indicating if the suggested activity makes you feel calm, energized, or is one that should be limited or avoided to reduce your stress.

SUGGESTED ACTIVITIES FOR PROPRIOCEPTIVE STIMULATION	CALMING	ENERGIZING	LIMIT OR AVOID
Yoga			
Running			
Swimming			
Dancing			
Weightlifting			
Stretching or Exercising			
Yardwork/ Mowing the Grass			
Vacuuming			
Woodworking			
Grocery Shopping			
Using a Weighted Blanket			
Getting a Massage			
Wearing a Jacket or Hat			
Using a Stress Ball			

Complete the chart below by listing the sensory events that shape your life. Indicate if they make you feel calm, energized, or if they should be limited or avoided to manage your stress.

ACTIVITIES YOU IDENTIFIED FOR VESTIBULAR STIMULATION	CALMING	ENERGIZING	LIMIT OR AVOID

THE TACTILE SYSTEM

This system detects light and firm touch, textures, pain, temperature, and vibration. Soft, hard, wet, dry, textured, smooth, gritty, or sticky are examples of encounters that stimulate the receptors.

The tactile system plays a vital role in our survival. It determines if a touch indicates a possible danger. This activates our fight or flight mode, producing chemicals that make us feel anxious.

Light touch encounters can be over-stimulating, activating our stress response. However, pleasant touch encounters contribute significantly to stress reduction, emotional security, and learning. These enjoyable touch encounters produce feel-good chemicals in the brain that soothe us.

 Complete the chart below by indicating if the suggested activity makes you feel calm, energized, or is one that should be limited or avoided to reduce your stress.

SUGGESTED ACTIVITIES FOR TACTILE STIMULATION	CALMING	ENERGIZING	LIMIT OR AVOID
Using a Stress Ball or Fidgets			
Holding Hands			
A Gentle Caress			
A Soft Blanket			
Taking a Shower or Bath			
Soaking your Feet			
Using Body Lotions			
Breeze from a Fan or the Wind			
Stroking a Pet			
Baking			
Gardening			
Pottery			
Fishing or Crabbing			
Vibrating Cushion			
Heating Pad			

Complete the chart below by listing the sensory events that shape your life. Indicate if they make you feel calm, energized, or if they should be limited or avoided to manage your stress.

ACTIVITIES YOU IDENTIFIED FOR VESTIBULAR STIMULATION	CALMING	ENERGIZING	LIMIT OR AVOID

THE VISUAL SYSTEM

This system detects colors, light, contrast, and movement. Flashing lights, designs, patterns, and moving objects stimulate these receptors.

Our ability to see helps us to process our environment and understand our world. It contributes to our sense of security by allowing us to see on-coming dangers.

Bright light, glare, busy patterns, and bright colors can over-stimulate people who have an over-sensitive system. The sensory overload can cause headaches, fatigue, and mood changes. People who are under-sensitive need intense visual stimulation to remain alert, attentive, and content.

 Complete the chart below by indicating if the suggested activity makes you feel calm, energized, or is one that should be limited or avoided to reduce your stress.

SUGGESTED ACTIVITIES FOR VISUAL STIMULATION	CALMING	ENERGIZING	LIMIT OR AVOID
Dimming the Lights			
Bright Lights			
Earth Tones			
Bright Colors			
Watching TV			
Playing Video Games			
Knick Knacks			
Drawing or Painting			
Watching Birds Fly			
Watching Fish Swim in Fish Tank			
People Watching			
Moving Objects			
Shopping			
Reading			
Playing Ball Games			

Complete the chart below by listing the sensory events that shape your life. Indicate if they make you feel calm, energized, or if they should be limited or avoided to manage your stress.

ACTIVITIES YOU IDENTIFIED FOR VESTIBULAR STIMULATION	CALMING	ENERGIZING	LIMIT OR AVOID

THE AUDITORY SYSTEM

This system detects the pitch, volume, tone, and rhythm of sounds. The receptors are stimulated by sounds, voices, music, and vibration. Hearing is our primary warning system to keep us safe. Hearing also allows us to communicate, learn, and enjoy the many wonderful sounds that life has to offer.

Auditory stimulation can have a lingering effect. People who have an under-sensitive system feel more organized and content when hearing sounds. This explains why they play the radio or TV when working. People who are over-sensitive may experience a sensory overload from sounds that are too loud or when there are too many noises to process. Signs of an auditory overload are headache, fatigue, mood changes, inability to concentrate, impulsiveness, and fidgeting.

 Complete the chart below by indicating if the suggested activity makes you feel calm, energized, or is one that should be limited or avoided to reduce your stress.

SUGGESTED ACTIVITIES FOR AUDITORY STIMULATION	CALMING	ENERGIZING	LIMIT OR AVOID
Invigorating Music			
Soft Rock			
Singing, Humming, or Whistling			
TV			
White Noise or Fan			
Silence			
Sound of Rain or Wind			
Laughter			
Podcasts			
Waterfall			
Ocean Waves			
Sound of Motors			
Meditation Tapes			

Complete the chart below by listing the sensory events that shape your life. Indicate if they make you feel calm, energized, or if they should be limited or avoided to manage your stress.

ACTIVITIES YOU IDENTIFIED FOR VESTIBULAR STIMULATION	CALMING	ENERGIZING	LIMIT OR AVOID

THE OLFACTORY SYSTEM

This system detects odors and determines if they are pleasant, toxic, or foul. The receptors are stimulated by perfumes, food odors, scented products, grass, exhaust, fire, and body odors.

The olfactory system is our most sensitive sensory system and helps us to detect danger. It helps us recognize familiar places and contributes to the flavor of the foods that we eat. Our sense of smell also plays a critical role in creating emotional memories.

Unlike our other senses, where stimulation produces a lingering effect, the benefits of olfactory inputs are only realized when the stimulus is present. Therefore, the scent must be noticeable to realize its benefit.

 Complete the chart below by indicating if the suggested activity makes you feel calm, energized, or is one that should be limited or avoided to reduce your stress.

SUGGESTED ACTIVITIES FOR OLFACTORY STIMULATION	CALMING	ENERGIZING	LIMIT OR AVOID
Air Fresheners			
Scented Candles			
Aromatherapy			
Essential Oils			
Perfumes or Cologne			
Scented Lotions			
Scented Products			
Bath Bombs			
Fresh Air			
Grass, Flowers, or Leaves			
Foods, Spices, or Coffee			
Campfires			

Complete the chart below by listing the sensory events that shape your life. Indicate if they make you feel calm, energized, or if they should be limited or avoided to manage your stress.

ACTIVITIES YOU IDENTIFIED FOR VESTIBULAR STIMULATION	CALMING	ENERGIZING	LIMIT OR AVOID

THE GUSTATORY SYSTEM AND ORAL STIMULATION

The gustatory system is responsible for detecting the five basic taste sensations: sweet, sour, bitter, salty, and umami (savory). This sense protects us from ingesting harmful substances, and it can be used to arouse or calm the nervous system.

 Complete the charts below by indicating if the suggested activity makes you feel calm, energized, or is one that should be limited or avoided to reduce your stress.

SUGGESTED ACTIVITIES FOR GUSTATORY STIMULATION	CALMING	ENERGIZING	LIMIT OR AVOID
Sweet Foods			
Sour Foods			
Bitter Foods			
Salty Foods			
Spicy Foods			
Savory Foods			
Minty Foods			
Mixed Flavors and Textures			

ACTIVITIES YOU IDENTIFIED FOR GUSTATORY STIMULATION	CALMING	ENERGIZING	LIMIT OR AVOID

SUGGESTED ACTIVITIES FOR ORAL STIMULATION	CALMING	ENERGIZING	LIMIT OR AVOID
Chewy Foods			
Crunchy Foods			
Chewing Gum or Hard Candy			
Using a Straw			
Hot Beverage			
Cold Beverage			
Ice Cream or Ice Pop			
Carbonated Drinks			
Humming or Whistling			

ACTIVITIES YOU IDENTIFIED FOR ORAL STIMULATION	CALMING	ENERGIZING	LIMIT OR AVOID

SENSE OF STABILITY

In this session, we will explore the importance of accurately identifying the intensity of your emotions. This will help you control your anxiety and emotional regulation. You will also evaluate your behaviors and reactions in situations that upset you to determine what triggered your response. This will help you identify what you wanted and how to manage your actions better in the future to achieve your goal.

SESSION GOALS:

☐ Review the discussion about Emotional Literacy to learn how to rate the intensity of feelings.

☐ Complete the *Self-Regulation Assessment* to identify how behaviors affect outcomes.

☐ Complete the *Emotional Control Assessment* to identify triggers of stress and your response to these stressors. This will help you learn to rate the intensity of your emotions so you can control them better in the future.

Please visit **http://www.SensoryAuthority.com/reader-bonus** to download additional copies of the therapeutic exercises contained in this book.

Life-Changing Moment...

IT ALWAYS COMES
DOWN TO TWO

Years ago, I went to Liberty State Park in Jersey City, New Jersey. This was before it was renovated to the beautiful park it is today. As I sat on one of the weathered railroad ties, I saw an older gentleman with a little white dog walking towards me. He smiled and said his name was John. He then started a conversation that I will never forget.

John talked about the weather and how he loved to bring his dog to the park. He said that he lived in Jersey City all his life and that he liked to make dollhouses for children as a hobby. John seemed happy and content, so you can only imagine my surprise when he stated that his wife had just died the day before.

He explained that they had been happily married for over 50 years and spoke of how much they loved each other. I was stunned. I could not understand how a man who had just lost his wife of over 50 years could be so happy. So, I gently said, "John, forgive me, but you seem incredibly happy for a man who just lost his wife."

John smiled and said, "I'm going to tell you something that you will never forget." He said, "God made everything simple. He made everything with two choices. We can choose to be happy, or we can choose to be sad. My wife is gone, and I will miss her with all my heart, but would it make any difference if I were sad? She would want me to be happy. If I were sad, it would only make things worse. It wouldn't bring her back, so I choose to be happy."

It was an interesting perspective. Then he said, "Don't make life more complicated than it needs to be. You see, there is up and down, day and night, healthy and sick, rich, and poor, smooth or bumpy, or on or off. Everything comes down to two." He then ended the conversation by saying, "Next time something bad happens in your life, ask yourself, will things be better if I am sad, or will they be better if I choose to be happy."

I left the park that day with a new perspective on life. This man was not saying that sorrow or depression is a choice; however, he was saying that we can make decisions that influence how we manage life's stressors. His words of wisdom have stayed with me over the years, and when hard times come, I choose to be happy. Truth be told, it does make things better.

Emotional Literacy: Rating Your Emotions

Our ability to correctly identify our emotions and react accordingly is regulated by our interoceptive system and is crucial for our success. This is the reason people joke about therapists always asking, 'And how did that make you feel?' This question encourages the client to identify the intensity of their emotions.

Emotions are formed through the information we receive through our external senses. This activates our inner senses to elicit a response.

For example, a situation may make your heartbeat faster, make your hands sweaty, and make it hard to breathe. This could indicate terror, excitement, or a surprise; therefore, the context in which we experience sensations must be considered.

The following chart provides an overview of our emotions. The intensity of each feeling increases from the bottom of the list to the top. Learning to identify your feelings accurately helps you respond to situations more appropriately in the future.

INTENSITY OF EMOTIONS

HAPPY	SAD	ANGRY	AFRAID	STRONG	WEAK	ASHAMED
Elated Thrilled Ecstatic	Hopeless Depressed Disappointed	Raging Furious Aggravated	Petrified Terrified Panicked	Powerful Forceful Determined	Helpless Overwhelmed Exhausted	Worthless Dishonored Sorrowful
Cheerful Satisfied Relieved	Distressed Melancholic Unhappy	Enraged Mad Upset	Frightened Intimidated Worried	Empowered Confident Energized	Drained Insecure Inadequate	Unworthy Defamed Sorry
Pleased Content Fine	Upset Gloomy Down	Frustrated Irritated Annoyed	Nervous Anxious Uneasy	Capable Sure Able	Incapable Unsure Shaky	Guilty Regretful Embarrassed

One, Two, Three

As you review the intensity of emotions, take a moment to think of three situations that make you feel happy, and three events that make you feel sad. Consider what sensory experiences are involved in each to determine their role in affecting your experience. This is not as easy as one might believe because we are often not consciously aware of our emotions. However, this activity will give insight that will help manage stressors.

The Power of Self-Reflection

Have you ever reacted to a situation, and upon looking back, you realized you responded inappropriately? Maybe you acted out because you wanted something or because someone upset you. Perhaps you were reacting to a situation nearby that did not directly involve you.

The following activity is truly life changing. It helps you recognize what you wanted, compared to what resulted from your behaviors, by determining if your actions helped you achieve your intended goal. This exercise will also help you identify what you were feeling at the time you acted out, providing insight to manage these challenging situations better in the future.

SELF-REGULATION ASSESSMENT

Reflect on an incident that upset you and caused you to respond inappropriately. Then evaluate the following to identify what triggered your stress, and the effect that resulted from you losing control of your emotions.

1. What was it that upset you?

A Threat	Action of Others	A Comment
A Commitment	Physical Touch	An Insult
A Disappointment	Lack of Time	Financial Situation

2. What were you feeling at the time?

Angry	Worried	Embarrassed	Scared	Overwhelmed	Protective
Tired	Confused	Unsafe	Frustrated	Unhappy	Misunderstood

3. How did you behave?

Yelled	Insulted Others	Cried	Threw Something	Hurt Others
Cursed	Threatened	Laughed	Hit Something	Hurt Self

4. What was it that you wanted?

Attention	To Be Left Alone	To Avoid Something
Help or Guidance	Have Things Your Way	Control of Situation
To Take a Break	To Feel Important	Have Your Opinion Heard
Safety	Peace	Respect

5. What was the result of your actions?

Made People Angry or Upset	Damaged Property	Lost Friends
Asked to Leave	Injured Others	Lost Job
Lost Privileges	Injured Self	Got in Trouble

6. How did your actions make other people feel?

Angry	Hurt	Confused	Scared
Upset	Worried	Sad	Frustrated

7. How should you have behaved to get what you wanted?

Asked for or Sought Out Help	Used Self-Talk or Calming Techniques
Used Words to Express Concern	Taken a Moment to Regroup

8. *What can you do to fix this problem?*

Apologize	Clean-up/Repair Damage	Accept Consequence
Talk it Over	Do Something Nice	Follow Directive

9. *What sensory encounters may have influenced your behavior?*

Noise	Temperature	Crowds	Felt Overwhelmed
Lighting	Time Constraints	Lack of Personal Space	Offensive Odors
Hunger or Thirst	Fatigue	Sickness	New Medication

Emotional Stability

Most of us are familiar with the Wong-Baker FACES pain scale rating system used by doctors to help patients rate their pain. The six faces each have an expression that corresponds with a pain level. Although they appear somewhat childish in design, these familiar emoji-type faces are an invaluable resource. They allow us to rate the intensity of our pain so we can monitor our symptoms.

The *Emotional Control Assessment* is similar in design to the Wong-Baker pain scale, but instead of using faces, it uses a numerical system to represent the intensity of your emotions. This system asks you to rate the level of your emotional control on a scale of 1—3.

Level 1—You are happy, content, and in control of your emotions.

Level 2—You are beginning to feel upset, frustrated, scared, or overwhelmed. This level is crucial for maintaining control of your emotions. The moment you recognize that a stressor is affecting your emotional well-being, you should implement a calming strategy to regain control.

Level 3—You feel angry, aggressive, and confrontational because you have lost control of your emotions. You need to recognize that your emotions are controlling you instead of you having control over your emotions. You need to implement some calming strategies to regain control as quickly as possible.

This rating system will help you identify situations that trigger your stress, so you can implement strategies to maintain control of your mood, temper, and behavior.

EMOTIONAL CONTROL ASSESSMENT

Complete the chart to identify the people, places, and circumstances that affect your emotional stability. This exercise will help you recognize stressors so you can avoid or manage them better in the future.

LEVEL 1 You feel content and in control. You are relaxed, confident, focused, happy, and calm.	List strategies that help you maintain a sense of calm. Make sure you include them on your Sensory Action Plan.
LEVEL 2 You are beginning to lose control of your emotions. You feel anxious, upset, irritated, confused, embarrassed, frustrated, scared, uncomfortable, or overwhelmed.	List situations that cause you to become upset and use your Sensory Action Plan to identify calming strategies.
LEVEL 3 You have lost control of your emotions and need to regain your composure. You feel angry, aggressive, impatient, adversarial, and confrontational.	List situations that triggered stress and use your Sensory Action Plan to identify calming strategies.

SENSORY RETREATS

Sensory retreats are used to relieve stress and improve concentration, but what exactly is a sensory retreat? A sensory retreat is when you reduce exposure to sensory inputs to give the nervous system time to rest. It is quite similar to sitting down to rest your body.

SESSION GOALS:

☐ Learn how sensory retreats help calm an over-stimulated nervous system.

☐ Learn how reducing sensory stimulation decreases anxiety and increases concentration.

☐ Follow the instructions for *Mindfulness with Progressive Muscle Relaxation* to experience the benefits of this popular practice.

☐ Complete the *Gratitude Journal* and *Stress Journals* to alleviate stress.

☐ Review Sensory-Focused Retreats and practice the suggested *Grounding Techniques*.

Please visit **http://www.SensoryAuthority.com/reader-bonus** to download additional copies of the therapeutic exercises contained in this book.

Sensory Overload

Have you ever seen a child have a temper tantrum or an adult who lashes out when they lose their temper? Quite often, this is a sign of sensory overload. Our emotions overflow when the nervous system is over-stimulated. The best solution for these situations is a sensory retreat.

Children who exhibit disruptive behaviors can be calmed when directed to a quiet space or calming corner. I am amazed at how quickly they regain control when given a few moments in a quiet environment to calm their nervous system. Adults also benefit from sensory retreats.

POINT TO PONDER...

Places like Disney World are fun and exciting, but they can also cause sensory overload. Children who lie down in the middle of the walkway, cry, or throw things, and adults who yell or lose their temper, are overwhelmed by the magnitude of sensory encounters.

The best solution for these behaviors is a sensory retreat. Retreat to a quiet location on the perimeter of the park, where sensory stimulation is reduced. This 'sensory retreat' gives the nervous system time to settle so that people can regain their composure. Today, many amusement parks, sports arenas, and restaurants have added sensory rooms where people of all ages can decompress.

Sensory Retreats for All Ages

It is important for people to understand how increasing or decreasing sensory inputs can enhance their lives. We all feel and perform our best when our sensory system is balanced. Sometimes we need more input to achieve that balance, and sometimes we need less. Have you ever noticed how creative thoughts or solutions to problems come to you when lying in bed or taking a shower? Inner thoughts surface when distractions are removed. Sensory retreats allow our thinking to become clearer and our emotions to become more regulated.

Adults are fortunate to have control over sensory events in their life. They can lower the volume if a sound is too loud or move away from an offensive touch or smell; however, there are times when adults experience sensory overload. There are several ways to limit sensory input and create a sensory retreat. You could go to a quiet place, take a drive in the car, go for a walk, take a bath, or relax in the pool. These activities limit specific sensory inputs, making us feel calmer, focused, and in control.

A Sensory Retreat for The Mind

Mindfulness, also known as meditation, is a popular sensory retreat. Sadly, some people shun this practice because of its association with Buddhism. Mindfulness is not about ideologies; it is the art of learning to limit life's distractions so you can connect with yourself.

I was once a skeptic myself until I experienced the effects of mindfulness. After one short session, I was surprised at how relaxed I felt. I quickly realized that my preconceived notions had prejudiced my thinking about the practice. This experience inspired me to learn more about it. If you share those same preconceived notions, I strongly encourage you to try mindfulness before rendering a final judgment.

There are many different types and methods of mindfulness. It is important to find the one that is right for you. They all help control the bombardment of stimulation to give the brain the much-needed rest it deserves. It helps you focus on internal, rhythmic sensory experiences, like breathing in and out to increase your attention, self-awareness, and peace of mind.

Benefits of Mindfulness

Mindfulness has been used for stress-reduction and self-development for many years. Studies suggest that it can also benefit many other areas of our life. It improves cognitive function, boosts the immune system, helps with weight management, and has been associated with benefits for healthy aging. It is also credited with controlling impulsive behaviors, improving emotional regulation, and helping with pain management.

Mindfulness with Progressive Muscle Relaxation

Mindfulness meditation is a psychological process that allows you to experience the present moment. It is no different than stopping to enjoy the scenery during a walk. This moment of pause lets you isolate your focus on the beauty of the landscape so you can savor the overall experience. Mindfulness helps you focus on the present moment without judgment or reaction to enjoy all that life has to offer.

How to Practice Mindfulness

Find a quiet place where you can sit comfortably with your arms relaxed at your side. Your posture should be upright but not rigid. You can close your eyes or fix your gaze on an object. You only need to invest as little as 10 to 20 minutes each day to enjoy the benefit of this practice.

Once you are comfortable, focus on each breath. Feel your breath as it enters and exits your body. Slowly breathe in, then slowly breathe out. As you continue this deep breathing, your mind should be focused on the air entering and exiting your body. You should now feel your body beginning to relax.

As you continue the deep breathing, focus your attention on your face. Take a deep breath in, and as you breathe out, relax the muscles of your face. You should feel the gentle release of each facial muscle. Continue this process for the rest of your muscles, working your way down your entire body. Each time you breathe in, you will concentrate on the specific muscles, and when you breathe out, feel your muscles release, and relax.

You should feel calm and peaceful as you continue the deep breathing. Allow positive thoughts to fill your mind as you breathe in and release any negative thoughts as you breathe out. Savor the feeling of your muscles relaxing. Slowly breathe in as you relish the moment of peace and tranquility, and then breathe out, releasing fear and doubt. You are now well prepared to start your day.

This is just one of many ways you can experience the peace and relaxation of mindfulness. Some people prefer guided meditation, while others prefer soothing music or tranquil sounds as they practice this art. Apps are available for those who prefer guided meditation, and classes are also available in most areas.

People who schedule a specific time each day to practice mindfulness find that having an established routine helps them maintain the practice. I encourage you to try mindfulness; you will be amazed at how it helps reduce stress and anxiety.

Journaling for Peace of Mind

Journaling provides numerous benefits, and it is an effective way to manage anxiety. It allows you to express your innermost thoughts, fears, conflicts, and ideas. It helps de-clutter your mind, so it is free of worries. Your journal should be private so that you can express yourself without fear of judgment from others.

When you invest time to organize your thoughts, it helps you solve problems and learn more about yourself. It also enables you to track progress, setbacks, and patterns in your life. Interestingly, people who journal say that their journal is their most trusted, non-judgmental friend.

The Gratitude Journal

A gratitude journal helps identify pleasurable moments in your life. It helps you appreciate special people and moments. Studies show that people who keep a gratitude journal are more optimistic and energized. They have less stress and improved sleep. Gratitude journals also help motivate and encourage you during difficult times.

Stress Journal

Stress journals allow you to release frustration by writing down what triggered your stress. It helps you identify triggers, patterns, or commonalities so that you can control stressors. For example, if you find that most of your stress originates at work, you need to modify that environment.

There are several other types of journals that can help people improve their lives. Prayer, workouts, ideas, projects, travel, and reading journals are examples of different journals that help reduce stress. Journal entries need not take long to complete; they are merely an outlet for you to express your thoughts and feelings to unburden your mind.

This program includes templates for a gratitude journal and stress journal. I strongly encourage you to try journaling. You may find the experience to be life changing.

GRATITUDE JOURNAL

A gratitude journal is used to document special people or situations that made your life better. It also includes a section to record things that you like about yourself. This helps you appreciate your valuable traits while improving your outlook on life and reducing stress.

DATE	SITUATIONS OR OPPORTUNITIES	PEOPLE	THINGS I HAVE	THINGS I LIKE ABOUT MYSELF

STRESS JOURNAL

This journal allows you to document situations that upset you, increasing your stress. It helps unburden your mind while identifying patterns of triggers so that you can take control over those stressors in the future.

DATE & TIME	TRIGGER	LOCATION	REACTION AND FEELINGS	HOW DID YOU RESPOND? Good, Fair, Poorly

Sensory-Focused Grounding Techniques

Sensory-focused grounding techniques help reduce anxiety by directing your attention to a specific sensory input. This limits distraction and allows you to connect with the present moment, preventing worries from consuming your mind. Some people find that wearing headphones in a dark room to focus on the music helps calm them, while others might relax by watching fish swim in a fish tank. There are countless ways that sensory events can be used to reduce stress and help organize our thoughts.

Sensory-focused techniques work well in most settings. They are a simple solution that solves a complex problem by allowing a person to regroup without calling attention to themselves. In practice, I instruct clients to use the following grounding techniques to reduce anxiety and prevent panic attacks.

Deep Breathing

Deep breathing is a simple exercise that has many benefits. It sends oxygenated air through your body, and it releases endorphins. This helps you focus, concentrate, and feel energized. It also helps reduce pain and stress while lowering your blood pressure. Deep breathing is a fast and easy sensory tool that can be used at any time. It is often used to calm people when they are feeling anxious, nervous, or frustrated.

Hot Coffee

One of the best ways to practice deep breathing is to *imagine* you are holding a cup of hot coffee. You start this exercise by slowly breathing in through your nose to 'smell' the rich aroma. You then pause before slowly blowing through your mouth as if you were trying to cool the hot drink. Repeat this cycle 5 to 7 times to reduce anxiety and stress.

Take Five to Survive

This exercise encourages you to focus on a specific activity to organize your thoughts and reduce anxiety. Begin by gently squeezing the top of your thumb as you think of one thing that you like to hear. It could be the sound of ocean waves, wind, music, or laughter. Then squeeze the top of your index finger and think of another sound. Continue until you get to your pinky. Start again, thinking of five things you like to see. Repeat this activity until you have named five items for each sense. This grounding technique helps you focus on pleasurable sensations, which produce feel-good chemicals in your brain.

I SPY

You can focus on the present moment and organize your thoughts by playing 'I Spy.' This helps to calm your nervous system by using your visual sense to locate a specific item. You can begin by finding five red items, five white items, five blue items, and so on. You can also modify this activity by looking for five things that are red, four that are blue, three that are white, two that are green, and one that is black. Any colors can be used for this exercise. You can also make it more challenging by looking for five things that start with the letter A, four that start with B, three that start with C, and so on. The exercise aims to direct your thoughts on the present moment, which helps calm anxiety.

Facial Expressions

Smile! Did you know that the first thing our eyes spot is a human face and that facial expressions impact on our emotional state? The tensing and releasing of facial muscles change the temperature of the blood flowing to our brain. It can raise or lower it. These temperature changes affect the part of the brain that regulates our emotions.

Facial expressions are also a form of communication, and we respond accordingly. If we see someone frown, we feel a sense of sadness. If we see someone smile, we feel happy. Therefore, it is important to surround yourself with smiling faces.

Choose a small happy picture of someone you care about and carry it in your wallet. When you start to feel anxious, look at the picture, and think of how that person looks, sounds, smells, and moves. I often recommend this activity for children who feel anxious in school. It has proven to be quite successful in calming their fears and increasing their attendance.

POINT TO PONDER...

Happy, smiling faces surround younger children. There are faces on their t-shirts, backpacks, stuffed animals, and in their picture books. Adults smile as they excitedly greet little children, but what happens when these smiling faces start to disappear as a child grows older? Is there a correlation between exposure to smiling faces, acceptance, and self-esteem?

Life-Changing Moment...

LAUGHTER IS THE BEST MEDICINE

Several years ago, my family and I went through some difficult times. My husband was injured in a near-fatal car crash. This traumatic event was frightening and stressful for my then 11, 12, and 13-year-old children. Less than a week after my husband came home from the hospital, I brought my daughter, Rachel, to the emergency room because she had a persistent headache that was worsening. I had attributed her symptoms to stress but quickly learned I was wrong.

The doctor admitted Rachel to the hospital because a pseudotumor was causing her headache. He explained that Rachel had excessive fluid in her brain, and the pressure could cause her to go blind. Our stress was indescribable. Rachel went on to endure years of suffering, not only from the recurring pseudo-tumor but also from severe gastroparesis. Her stomach stopped functioning, so she could no longer eat a regular diet. During these years of distress, the only thing that brought her joy was the Ellen show.

Ellen DeGeneres could make Rachel smile, even in her darkest hours. I thanked God that her comedic style lifted my daughter's spirits. At that time, I had no way of knowing that Ellen would also help my son during his frightening health crisis that lay ahead.

Approximately one year after Rachel's diagnosis, my oldest son was diagnosed with a rare skin cancer. We sat in silence in the hospital, waiting to meet the surgeon who would hopefully save his arm. Across the room sat a woman whose face was severely injured. You could tell she had no distinguishable nose. Her dazed husband held her in his arms as they quietly waited for their turn. The only sign of life in this tension-filled waiting room was a small TV.

Words could never describe my joy when the Ellen show came on. Ellen opened with a hysterical monologue. The frowns in that room quickly changed into smiles as hints of laughter filled the air. My young son was laughing then, my husband laughed. The woman with the severely injured face was even trying to smile. At that moment, I was overwhelmed with gratitude, knowing that Rachel was home smiling and laughing too.

My family survived those stressful years through faith in God and the support of family and friends. We also found strength by watching gifted people who made us laugh when everything around us made us want to cry. Humor and laughter played a significant role in our healing. And today, all these years later, words cannot describe the joy I feel when Rachel calls and says, "Hey Mom, did you see Ellen today?"

Sense of Humor

It is often said that laughter is the best medicine. Our sense of humor is just as important as our other senses. Studies show that laughter has short-term and long-term benefits: it can reduce pain, boost your immune system, and improve your mood and self-regulation. When you laugh, you fill your body with oxygen-rich air, which energizes your cardiovascular system and stimulates your muscles. Your body also produces endorphins, which reduces pain, manages stress, and fosters social attachments.

People will sometimes feel like they have lost their sense of humor. Depression, loss of a loved one, stressful events, and certain medical conditions can dampen this sense, but not unlike our other senses, you have to nurture this sense-ability. You can start by finding funny pictures that make you smile and place them where they can be seen. Even if they do not produce a belly laugh, they stimulate your sense of humor.

Some people watch funny movies or TV shows. If one silly joke causes them to smile, they are stimulating their sense of humor. There are also websites or joke books that offer a good laugh or two. A sense of humor can be quite healing. It reduces stress as it helps us cope with our imperfections. And sometimes, a good laugh at the right moment can change everything, so do not ever believe that you've lost your sense of humor: It is never lost—it just needs to be nurtured.

SENSE OF TIME

Chronoception is the inner sense that detects the passage of time. This system can be under- or over-sensitive, much like our other sensory systems. In this session, you will explore how you are spending your time and identify the time of day when you feel most stressed. You will also learn how to budget your time to be more productive.

SESSION GOALS:

☐ Review Sense of Time to discover the importance of time management.

☐ Complete the *Time Analysis* to determine how you are spending your time. Highlight the times you felt anxious, upset, or overwhelmed. This will help you identify triggers.

☐ Review Environmental Stressors and complete the *Time and Place* worksheet to identify the time and encounters contributing to your stress.

☐ Review the Science of Problem Solving and complete *Effective Problem-Solving* exercise to establish a plan for solving future problems.

Please visit **http://www.SensoryAuthority.com/reader-bonus** to download additional copies of the therapeutic exercises contained in this book.

Life-Changing Moment...

IT'S ABOUT TIME

It was time to take another test in college. As the professor handed out the exam, she announced that we had 60 minutes to complete all the questions. Then she said, "And Judi, do not ask anyone what the date is today because you should know it, and I might just start grading you on it." I could hear my classmates giggle, but the professor was not joking.

My heart started to race, and I broke out in a cold sweat. Once again, I had no idea what day it was, and I even struggled to recall the month. This was not new to me because I have always had a diminished sense of time. It may sound funny at first until you consider how a sense of time affects your life. It is hard to remember birthdays or holidays. It is also difficult to estimate how long it will take to complete a task or how long it will take to get somewhere.

Thankfully, my sense of time has slowly improved over the years, and although I have struggled with time concepts, I never underestimated the value of time. I am fully aware that time and money are both commodities. You can make more money, but you cannot make more time.

I try to invest my time wisely each day by limiting things like social media or watching TV. Although these things can be intriguing, they can distract me from working toward my goals. It is important to be aware of how you spend your time because you never get it back once it is gone.

Sense of Time

Have you ever wondered how some people find time to be successful in their careers and still have time to do the things they love? These people have learned how to manage one of life's most valuable resources, time. Most people learned the value of a dollar and how to budget, spend, or invest it, but they were never taught how to manage their time. People often look at the clock and wonder, 'Where did the time go?' We have all experienced these moments. Perhaps the reason the concept of time is difficult to manage is that it is not tangible. There is nothing concrete to see or hold, so it seems limitless, but it is important to learn to manage your time, so you can enjoy all that life has to offer.

How Long is 3 Minutes?

The concept of time is unique to each person. One study proved this by asking participants to shout 'stop' when they believed 3 minutes had passed. They were told they could not look at the clock and to continue what they were doing during this time. Interestingly, the study found that the concept of time varies by age and that people in their twenties were the most accurate in determining when 3 minutes had passed.

Intrigued by this work, we conducted a similar study with our clients to better understand how they perceived time. The results were astounding: some clients shouted 'stop' after 2 minutes, while most of those tested yelled it at 4 minutes. One person did not say 'stop' until 6 minutes had passed. This clinical observation confirmed that the concept of time varies between people of all ages. It helps explain why people become anxious when told, 'We're leaving in 5 minutes,' because what seems like 5 minutes to one person seems like 2 minutes to another. This is the reason that occupational therapists often recommend using a free visual timer app on phones because it helps with time concepts.

Where Did the Time Go?

For the next activity, you will document how you spend your time each day over one week. As you record your daily activities on the Time Analysis Worksheet, it is important that you highlight the times when you feel anxious. This will help determine what circumstances or sensory encounters trigger your stress (See Figure 1).

TIME	SUNDAY
7:00—8:00	Gym
8:00—9:00	Drove home/Took a shower
9:00—10:00	Church
10:00—11:00	Grocery shopping
11:00—12:00	Put food away/Made lunch

Example (Figure 1)

In this example, the client indicated that grocery shopping in the morning triggered stress. This allows them to analyze the environment during that time of day to determine what modifications can be made to reduce stress. It may have been the lights, sounds, or the challenge of locating items on the shelf. It could also have been odors or temperature changes, but it is often the fear of seeing people they know. Spontaneous encounters can elicit social anxiety. Shopping early in the morning or late evening can help reduce social encounters because the stores are not as busy.

TIME ANALYSIS

 Document how you spend your time each day, highlighting the times when you felt anxious.

	SUNDAY	MONDAY	TUESDAY	WEDNESDAY	THURSDAY	FRIDAY	SATURDAY
Date							
5:00 AM							
6:00 AM							
7:00 AM							
8:00 AM							
9:00 AM							
10:00 AM							
11:00 AM							
NOON							
1:00 PM							
2:00 PM							
3:00 PM							
4:00 PM							
5:00 PM							
6:00 PM							
7:00 PM							
8:00 PM							
9:00 PM							
10:00 PM							
11:00 PM							
MIDNIGHT							

Time Analysis Review

After you have completed the time analysis, determine how much time you invested in the following:

Personal Care: Personal hygiene, grooming, eating, and exercise.

Responsibilities: The obligation of caring for children, pets, financial matters, etc.

Work: Responsibilities for paid employment or volunteer services.

Education: Formal education or informal learning.

Relaxation/Leisure: Activities you find enjoyable.

Social Participation: In-person engagement with family, friends, etc.

Social Media: Facebook, Instagram, Snapchat, etc.

Sleep: Your ability to sustain sleep and restore energy.

Spiritual: Time devoted to spiritual growth and enlightenment.

Did you spend too much time on social media, playing video games, or watching TV? Perhaps you spent most of your time working or sleeping. It is important to review how you used your time, so you can learn to use it more efficiently in the future.

Life-Changing Moment...

ANALYZING ACTIVITIES

When I first met Danny, whose words inspired the creation of this program, he battled drug addiction. He had turned to drugs, hoping to ease the pain of anxiety. In an effort to help him identify the situations that triggered his stress, I would have him review his day hour by hour. He would start with his waking hour and discuss each of his activities, while analyzing the sensory events' role on his anxiety. The insight gleaned from this type of analysis is amazing.

Danny candidly shared all aspects of his life, and in listening to him speak, I quickly realized that Danny was a craver. He craved touch, sounds, sights, smells, taste, and movement. He had a sensory appetite that seemed almost insatiable. This caused me to wonder what role sensory encounters had on his behaviors.

For instance, when discussing mealtimes, Danny stated that he needed foods to be spicy and colorful, or he would feel discontent and frustrated. He needed the room to be bright and rich with sounds, or he would feel anxious. He also mentioned that he needed a seat at the end of the table so he could easily get up and move around. I found this remarkably interesting and asked him how he would feel if he were to dine in a quiet restaurant with dim lighting and served bland foods. He replied, 'Stressed.'

Unfortunately, people do not always recognize the role that a sensory event has on stress. People tend to say they had a bad day, lumping every circumstance together. However, when they learn to analyze their activities to identify which sensory event triggered their anxiety, they can take steps to change it.

The ability to identify sensory needs is quite significant. It allows people to recognize how every situation throughout the day has the potential to become a stressor due to too much or too little of a sensory input. This awareness enables the person to pinpoint the root cause of their anxiety.

Environmental Stressors

People often come to therapy, stating they had a bad day. When we systematically review what happened during the day, we can pinpoint the situations that increased stress. This helps identify stressors so that they can be managed in the future.

Some people feel anxious at the start of the day. It could be caused by the smell of bacon and eggs cooking or everyone talking. For others, stress may start later, when they were squished between commuters on the subway or overwhelmed by the bright lights in the office.

It is important to learn to identify the time of day and circumstances that trigger anxiety. The next therapeutic exercise helps you evaluate these factors, revealing the sensory encounters contributing to your stress. This insight enables you to take steps to control it.

POINT TO PONDER...

I once treated a teenage boy who would come home from school upset. The teacher told his parents that their son would get mad and storm out of class. After completing his time analysis worksheet, we were able to pinpoint that his day was good until he had science class. We then reviewed each of the senses which helped to determined that his stress was triggered by the noise from a loud group of kids in the class and from having to huddle close together to complete experiments. This enabled us to make some simple modifications that helped him significantly.

If are you having trouble pinpointing the cause of your stress, perhaps completing the time analysis worksheet will help you discover the source of your frustration.

TIME AND PLACE

 Review the highlighted entries on your Time Analysis and use the chart below to identify the specific sensory encounters that made you feel anxious.

TIME AND ENVIRONMENT/ WHAT MADE YOU FEEL ANXIOUS	SIGHTS	SOUNDS	SMELLS	TOUCH	TASTE
Example: Sunday 10 am Grocery shopping	Bright, busy, and too much to look at. Too many sounds. Smell from seafood department. Touching the slimy packages of meat.				

Upon completing this exercise, you should have a better understanding of the exact situations and sensory encounters that contribute to your stress. You may also find that you feel more anxious in the morning or as the day goes on. This insight enables you to control and manage these stressors in the future.

Life-Changing Moment...

DON'T MAKE A PROBLEM BIGGER

Years ago, I worked in a store located in an affluent town in New Jersey. Many of the customers were successful, influential people that were well-known throughout the country. To me, they were just friendly customers who were a part of my everyday life. One day, a customer invited me to go motorcycle riding with him. He said it was part of a 'poker run' with Malcolm Forbes. At the time, I did not know much about Mr. Forbes, but it sounded fun, so I agreed to go.

When I arrived at the Forbes estate, I was surprised at the number of people participating in the event. Mr. Forbes was extremely generous, allowing people to use his motorcycles for these events. I savored the entirety of this moment: the friendly people who wore the bright red vest that read 'Capitalist Tools' on the back, the shiny, new motorcycles, and the thunderous roar of the bike's engines.

One by one, the motorcycles formed a line, traveling over hills and roadways in this orderly fashion. It was so much fun, and when I thanked Mr. Forbes for giving me this opportunity, he graciously invited me to ride with him again. I enjoyed many more poker runs with him over the next several months, but I vividly remember one. The bike leading our group that day accidentally made an illegal turn, and naturally, we all followed. Sirens sounded as over thirty motorcycles were instructed to pull over on a busy highway's narrow shoulder.

In confusion, I exited on the wrong side of the bike. The hot exhaust pipe burned through my jeans, burning my lower calf. Mr. Forbes looked at the wound and said that the wind from riding would help ease the pain. He was right: when we were riding, the pain was tolerable, but when we stopped, the pain was intense.

Upon arriving back at his estate, I limped over to thank Mr. Forbes for his generosity. Perplexed, he asked why I was limping. I reminded him that I had burned my leg. In a slightly serious tone, he asked if I had also hurt my knee. I said, "No, I only burned my leg." He then asked why I was limping if I had not hurt my knee. He raised a good point, but before I could respond, he said, "Don't make a problem bigger than it is. Your burn will feel better in a few hours, but you can still bend your knee to walk." I was embarrassed because I knew he was right. There was no reason to limp or to make a problem bigger than it needs to be.

The Science Behind Problem Solving

What creates a problem? Problems are barriers that prevent us from achieving a goal. They are often caused by a conflict in values, resources, plans, or aspirations. For example, there might be a conflict between your income and the money needed to pay the rent, or a conflict between your job and childcare. Everyone has problems, yet little time is spent teaching people how to solve them effectively. The next therapeutic activity teaches you how to analyze and solve problems using an easy to follow format.

EFFECTIVE PROBLEM SOLVING

 Choose a problem that you recently encountered and complete the problem-solving worksheet.

Step 1: Identify the problem.

What is the problem?	
Why is this a problem?	
What caused the problem?	
Who else does this problem affect?	
When must it be solved?	
What will improve if you find a solution?	
What would happen if the problem remains?	

Step 2: How big is this problem?

On a scale of 1—5, with five representing a complex problem, rate the intensity of this problem. Consider if this problem will have a significant long-term effect on your life or create a short-term inconvenience.

This problem is a _____ on the scale of 1—5.

5   **Emergency: Danger, fire, accident**
4   **Gigantic Problem: Very important/Maximum impact on life**
3   **Big Problem: Quite important/Significant impact on life**
2   **Medium Problem: Important. Some impact on life**
1   **Little Problem: Not too important. Minimal impact**

Step 3: Solution checklist:

- ☐ Did you brainstorm ideas with others and consider past situations?
- ☐ Did you generate alternate solutions options?
- ☐ Did you envision the cause and effect of each solution?
- ☐ Are you willing to accept responsibility for the outcome of the solution?

On the chart below, list the following:

Possible Solutions	
Possible Benefits to Solution	
Possible Risk or Consequence from Solution	
Who Will Benefit from This Solution	
Date to Implement Solution	

SENSE OF SELF

In this session, you will explore how roles create your identity and how they can impact your ability to tolerate sensory encounters. You will also learn how motivators, governed by your inner senses, and values affect decision making.

SESSION GOALS:

☐ Complete the *Identifying Your Roles* worksheet to learn how roles create your identity. Examine how your role responsibilities impact your tolerance of sensory stimuli.

☐ Complete the *Identifying Your Values* worksheet to identify the values that are most important to you. Consider how these values guide your actions.

☐ Review the Science of Motivation and Values to distinguish the difference between intrinsic and extrinsic motivation.

☐ Review the *Science of Decision-Making* and complete the *Decision-Making Planner* to refine your decision-making skills.

Please visit **http://www.SensoryAuthority.com/reader-bonus** to download additional copies of the therapeutic exercises contained in this book.

Life-Changing Moment...

ONLY A SOLDIER KNOWS

He is 99 years old and has been married to the love of his life for over 75 years. He is a husband, father, son, brother, cousin, grandfather, great-grandfather, uncle, neighbor, and friend. He is also a business owner, volunteer at his church, and he is a veteran. Many years ago, he was a soldier in the United States Air Force. While there, he served as a tail gunner in World War II. He created a lifetime of memories with the people that he loves, yet not a day goes by when he does not mention the war.

As he shares the stories of those difficult times, listeners can only imagine what he saw, heard, smelled, touched, and felt. Try as they will, only the surviving members of his unit can genuinely understand the sensory experiences they encountered there and how those experiences impacted their lives.

Each year, the brave men from his unit meet and reminisce about their role as American soldiers. They are the only ones who can fully appreciate what was expected of them. They are also the only ones who experienced the same sights, sounds, and smells during those frightening days far from home. Only other soldiers can identify with the impact that war had on their life.

This is similar to how only mothers can fully understand motherhood's sensory experiences, pregnancy, labor and delivery, sleepless nights, and consoling a crying baby. Only firefighters can fully appreciate the senses involved in fighting a fire: the heat from the blaze, the cries for help, and the strength required to save others.

Our unique roles form our identity, and they affect our perception of sensory encounters. This commonality allows us to bond with others who share the same roles, helping to create our social circles. Commonality fosters inclusion and a sense of community. This sense of belonging reduces stress and increases one's self-esteem. This is why it is important to identify the roles we have in life.

The Science of Roles and Identity

How we perceive our identity has a profound impact on our beliefs and behaviors. Studies have found that different types of identities shape our lives. There is a personal identity, role-based identity, and social identity, as defined below:

- **Personal Identity**: Created by our name, birthdate, race, attributes, characteristics, and knowledge learned through life experiences.

- **Role-based Identity**: Created through a position in our social structure that involves at least one other person. The expectations of these roles are socially defined and scripted. For example, if you are a parent, this role helps define your identity, sense of self, and self-worth.

- **Social Identity**: This identity is created through our sense of belonging to a group that shares similar values, goals, or life experiences. Social identity sometimes relies on the 'us or them' way of thinking.

If you belong to a church, you share their social identity. Your profession is another example of a social group. Sometimes, we belong to a social group that we did not choose. For example, families who lost a child to cancer now belong to the group of families who suffered a similar loss. Although this group membership is not of their choosing, it still contributes to their identity.

It is important to consider the following when discussing roles:

- **Role Conflict**: This occurs when you have a conflict between two roles. For instance, if you happen to be the coach of a baseball team and you are the father of one the players, you may experience a conflict in the two roles when assigning positions or playing time. These types of conflicts increase stress.

- **Role Ambiguity**: This occurs when the expectations of your role are not clearly defined. This creates uncertainty, which creates anxiety and heightens stress.

- **Role Expectation**: This is how other people believe one should behave in a role. This increases stress because it is hard to live up to other people's standards.

- **Role Stress**: The stress that results from feeling pressured to fulfill certain expectations in a role.

Sometimes we assume a role based on labeling or stereotyping. If we were to say, 'Tom has a problem with addiction,' we would be placing value on Tom being a person who suffers from a condition. However, if we said, 'Tom is an addict,' this would define Tom by society's depiction of someone who is addicted to drugs. This type of labeling places value on the condition rather than on the person. This stereotyping also happens to people who have autism, diabetes, or other conditions. Therefore, we should be mindful of how labels affect a person's identity. It can also be difficult to realize where one role ends, and another begins. This happens when we act more like a parent than a sibling, or more like a friend than a boss.

As you continue to develop your sensory profile, you will start to recognize how roles impact your perception and tolerance of sensory experiences. For example, as a parent, you may not be bothered by the sound of your child's cry; however, you may feel annoyed by the sound of other children crying. If you typically avoid touch encounters, you may find that these encounters do not bother you when you are in a caregiver role. And if you dislike heights and avoid climbing ladders, you may find that climbing a ladder is tolerable when helping your aging father replace burnt-out bulbs in the overhead light. Although the expectations associated with a role can sometimes expose us to sensory encounters that increase our anxiety, there are also times when our roles help us tolerate sensory experiences.

Life-Changing Moment...

TRUE TO OUR CHARACTER

A few years ago, my niece, Kristen, moved to Nashville and married a musician named, Schylar. This young couple has a great relationship as they share many things in common. They are both fun, likable people; and together, they own Sky Studios in Brentwood, Tennessee. There they help aspiring musicians develop their talent and pursue their dreams.

Kristen and Schylar also share a love of fashion, favoring trendy clothes, adorned with sunglasses, scarves, and hats. However, Kristen feels most comfortable when dressing for an occasion, while Schylar prefers to maintain his fashionable style.

One day, while preparing to attend a family outing, Schylar contemplated what he should wear. Perhaps jeans and a t-shirt would be deemed most appropriate, but after careful consideration, he decided to dress in his usual chic style—a decision he would never regret.

As they headed to the party, they made a quick stop at a local food store where a man approached them, saying how much he loved Schylar's outfit. To their surprise, it was Steven Tyler from the band, Aerosmith. Mr. Tyler spent several minutes discussing Schylar's wardrobe and fashion accessories. Schylar was so excited; he gave Mr. Tyler his favorite pair of sunglasses. It was a priceless moment that they will never forget.

When Schylar recalls that memorable day, he reflects on the fact that if he had not been true to his character by dressing in his preferred style, he would have missed that memorable moment. He says, "I would have been just another guy in jeans and a t-shirt, shopping for food."

I wonder how many special moments we miss when we are not true to our character?

Sense of Identity

Throughout the day, we are continually assuming different roles. It is important to recognize how the expectations for each role impacts our life. For example, if you are a passenger in a car and ask the driver to slow down, it will have a vastly different impact than if a police officer tells that driver to 'slow down.' This is similar to a parent asking their child, 'Did you do your homework yet?' as opposed to a friend asking that same question. Every role comes with expectations, and those expectations can increase our stress.

IDENTIFY YOUR ROLES

Review the list below and highlight your current roles. Determine if your roles are exposing you to sensory encounters that increase your stress. If so, determine what modifications you can make to limit your exposure to the offensive source. For example, if you crave movement, but your job requires you to sit at your desk for most of your shift, you may find that using a chair that swivels significantly reduces stress. You could also schedule periodic movement breaks to meet your sensory needs. It is important to recognize how roles affect our ability to control sensory encounters and how they also influence our ability to tolerate them.

Mother/Father	Son/Daughter	Aunt/Uncle	Friend	Cousin
Husband/Wife	Boyfriend/Girlfriend	Grandparent	Student	Caregiver
Employer	Employee	Co-Worker	Legal Authority	Teacher
Coach	Mentor/Leader	Provider	Driver	Soldier
Pastor	Parishioner	Athlete	Spectator	Public Speaker

You may find that some of your role responsibilities conflict with your sensory profile. For example, your job may require you to attend busy events with large crowds, but you may be over-sensitive to loud noise and touch experiences. It is crucial to identify how sensory encounters related to roles are impacting your life. It is also important to define your values and assess what motivates you to behave in a particular manner.

The Science of Motivation and Values

Intrinsic motivation is when the drive to do something comes from within. It produces a sense of pride, accomplishment, and purpose. For instance, I study hard in school because I want to learn.

Extrinsic motivation is when motivation comes from an external source. This includes rewards, praise, or acceptance, but it could also be fear of punishment or disproval. For example, I work hard in school to get good grades (a positive reward); or I work hard to get good grades so my parents will not punish me (a negative result).

Extrinsic motivators can expose us to sensory experiences that cause anxiety by prompting us to put ourselves in uncomfortable situations to please our boss, relative, or friend. We try to tolerate large crowds, dark places, or other undesired sensory encounters to avoid repercussions, which is why we should consider motivators when evaluating sensory encounters.

Values will also guide our actions by defining what is important. When there is a conflict in values, it creates inner turmoil, which increases anxiety. Therefore, it is essential to identify our values and recognize how they affect our roles, relationships, decisions, and behaviors.

IDENTIFYING YOUR VALUES

 Review the list below and highlight the values that are important to you.

Honesty	Kindness	Loyalty	Trust	Independence
Family	Faith	Friendship	Patience	Gratitude
Love	Commitment	Freedom	Happiness	Sincerity
Generosity	Unity	Humility	Knowledge	Education
Perseverance	Health	Equality	Vitality	Community
Prosperity	Shrewdness	Perfection	Winning	Success
Wealth	Status	Obedience	Popularity	Power
Professionalism	Diversity	Bravery	Respect	Control
Modesty	Inner Peace	Simplicity	Creativity	Nature
Sexiness	Fun	Achievement	Fame	Appearance

Life-Changing Moment...

INTUITION SAVED MY LIFE

Years ago, I made a decision that saved my life, though I could not have known it at the time.

When I was in my late teens, I worked in a retail store. One warm day, I decided I would go to the reservoir after work. The beach there was scenic and secluded. Excitedly, I shared these plans with the customers. When my shift ended, I put on my flip flops and hurried to the door. In my haste, I caught my toe on the door jam and immediately felt a surge of pain. I knew the toe was broken, but I was determined to go to the beach anyway.

As I approached the highway, I wanted to turn right toward the beautiful reservoir, but the pain in my foot prompted me to turn left toward my home. As I was driving, I heard a car beeping its horn and noticed the driver was smiling and waving to me. Naturally, I smiled and waved back, thinking I knew him. The driver repeated this several more times over the next 10 miles. The man did not look familiar, so I took an earlier exit, hoping to avoid him, but he followed me up the ramp. He then parked his car in front of mine to prevent me from leaving.

The well-groomed, professionally dressed man approached me with a big smile on his face. Normally, I would open my door to introduce myself, but the situation was unnerving, so I locked the doors and opened my window ever so slightly. The man smiled and asked me out for a drink. When I refused, he turned away, but when he looked back, something had drastically changed.

The expression on his face was frightening. His smile was gone, and his voice was now stern and deliberate. Instinctively, I made a critical decision to throw the car into reverse and back down the ramp to the busy highway. The man had not said anything intimidating, but my intuition prompted me to react.

The next day, a local police officer happened to stop by my store to get coffee. I told him about the man who had followed me home from work and he informed me that they had been looking for a man who fit this description.

He was wanted for recently attacking a woman and for killing two women years earlier at a beach. When they showed me the picture, I knew it was him. We realized he must have overheard my plans about going to the reservoir, making me a perfect target.

After a nightmarish few months, the man was apprehended. I have often thought about that day and how my senses detected inconsistencies that prompted me to take flight. I am fortunate that intuition saved my life. Intuition is an invaluable resource that should not be ignored when making decisions.

Every Decision Changes Your Life

What should I wear today? Should I accept or decline this invitation? A decision must be made when we must choose between one or more options. Every decision we make is influenced by our sensory needs and has an impact on our lives.

Decisions require deductive reasoning, but they also rely on internal cues known as intuition. Intuition is a subconscious way of thinking, formed from past experiences, observing others in similar situations, and our values. For example, if a friend asks you to call out of work to go to the beach with them, you now have a decision to make. You may want to go to the beach because you long to feel the hot sun against your skin as you listen to the sound of the waves, but the conflict between your values and your desires makes you feel queasy. Your inner senses are warning you that you might be risking your job if you call out of work.

Your roles, values, sensory preferences, and internal sensations influence your decision-making. If you value fun more than honesty, you may choose to go to the beach. If you value honesty and reliability more than fun, your inner senses will direct you to go to work. Deductive reasoning also helps to guide our decisions. It is a structured approach that considers all possibilities to reach a conclusion. It is important to occasionally review decision-making strategies because every decision we make affects our life.

The Science of Decision-Making

The process of deciding requires a careful analysis of every option. Please take a moment to review this process. It will guide you toward making the best decisions.

Step 1: Determine which decision must be made first.

One decision creates another. For example, if you called out of work to go to the beach, what beach would you go to, and what excuse would you give your boss?

Step 2: Rate the importance of this decision on a scale of 1 to 3:

1—This decision will have a minimal benefit or consequence in my life.

2—This decision will have a short-term benefit or consequence that will impact my life.

3—This decision will have long-term benefits or consequences that will significantly impact my life and well-being.

What rating would you give calling out of work to go to the beach? How much of an impact can this have on your life?

Step 3: Evaluate the pros and cons of each option.

List the pros and cons of each option. Consider what message your inner senses are telling you and visualize the benefits or consequences of your decision. Decisions affect safety, relationships, and trustworthiness, along with many other areas of life. Your choices will also impact others. For example, if you call out of work, your co-workers will have to do your job.

Step 4: Make your decision.

After reviewing the pros and cons, determine the best option for your decision.

Step 5: Review your decision.

Review your decision. If it is not producing the desired results, modify your actions.

Decisions can have a lasting effect. They produce either a positive or negative outcome. Planning your decisions does not guarantee that things will turn out as you anticipated; however, it helps you determine possible outcomes to make the best decision. This will help reduce or eliminate stressful situations in your life.

THE DECISION-MAKING PLANNER

Use this planner to determine the best possible outcome when making decisions.

1. What decision do you have to make? Rate the importance on a scale of 1-3: _____

2. List the possible options and narrow your choices down to two:

3. Complete the pros and cons chart for each option. Take into consideration your values and how the decision can impact your life.

WILL IT IMPROVE OR RISK MY…	PROS FOR OPTION 1 / OPTION 2	CONS FOR OPTION1 / OPTION 2
Safety		
Health		
Employment		
Relationships		
Finances		
Time		

4. Reflect on lessons learned from past experiences.

_____

_____

_____

_____

5. Determine if you can change your decision or if it is a final decision.

_____

_____

_____

6. Ask yourself if you are prepared to take responsibility for your decision.

_____

_____

_____

Decision-making skills can help you determine where to live, what job to take, and whom to marry. It can also help you in many other areas of your life.

SENSE OF ACCOMPLISHMENT

Successful people often attribute much of their success to the role models who influenced their lives. In this session, you will explore how role models shape your life and how your sensory preferences impact career choices.

SESSION GOALS:

☐ Review the importance of role models and how their example influences your decisions and behaviors.

☐ Complete the *Who Are Your Role Models* exercise to identify the character traits you admire.

☐ Review How Sensory Preferences Affect Career Choices and complete the *Career Path Assessment* to determine how your sensory profile impact your career choices.

☐ Complete the *Professional Performance Assessment* to identify strengths and areas that require further development.

Please visit **http://www.SensoryAuthority.com/reader-bonus** to download additional copies of the therapeutic exercises contained in this book.

Life-Changing Moment...

ROLE MODELS

When our son, Harry, was accepted to Cornell University, we were thrilled. He had confidently prepared for this new venture, but upon arriving at campus, something changed. He started to question his abilities as he interacted with the other students. He expressed this concern as we gathered in the crowded auditorium for orientation. There it quickly became apparent that our son was not the only student experiencing this moment of trepidation.

We stood in the back of the room as the staff introduced the keynote speaker. It was accomplished alumnus, Mr. Dave Price. He looked familiar as he coolly took the stage. I asked, "Isn't that the meteorologist on NBC?" Someone replied, "Yes. He's a Cornell graduate who comes back each year to welcome the incoming class." Immediately, we found comfort in seeing his familiar face. Mr. Price's confident, laid-back demeanor was refreshing in this tense atmosphere of uncertainty. He then greeted the crowd with a smile and shared his story, inspiring everyone with his life-changing words.

With a comedic flair, Mr. Price spoke about his years at Cornell. He talked about his heart-wrenching moments of defeat, his most embarrassing moments, and his successes. One minute he had people laughing, and the next, he brought them to tears. He quickly gained the respect of everyone in attendance, and he used that authority to encourage the students on their journey.

His presentation was not only entertaining and informative; it was unforgettable. Over the next few years, my son and I would often reflect on his insightful narrative, finding strength and guidance from his experiences. His words proved to be a beacon of hope to my son during many arduous times at Cornell.

Words could never convey our gratitude or the admiration we feel for Mr. Price. His heartfelt account of life at Cornell became the cornerstone of my son's collegiate success. However, Mr. Price did not only motivate the incoming students that day; his speech inspired me as well. I was impressed by his communication style and how he used real-life stories to connect with his audience. I also admired his ability to communicate strength, vulnerability, and leadership with his words. Since hearing him speak, I look to him as a role model and try to emulate his communication style when teaching people about the wonderful world of sensory processing.

Role Models

Have you ever thought about who influences your decisions and the reason why you chose that person? A role model is someone you admire, who inspires you to be like them, so you imitate their behaviors. They may be family members, people we know, or people that we have never personally met. Relatives, co-workers, teachers, celebrities, or other successful people are often referred to as role models.

My parents have both been wonderful role models for my family and for people who know them. They embrace faith, compassion, kindness, and an appreciation for learning. They also value hard work, perseverance, and generosity. I have learned by their example and incorporate their values in all that I do.

Role models are fundamental to our self-development and goal attainment. They impact our behaviors and decisions, and they play an integral role in cultivating our future. Positive role models are respected people who emulate the values and achievements that we admire. We are inspired by their courage, work ethic, skills, or other notable qualities, and we look to their example to direct our path.

Role Models Are Not Perfect

We choose role models because of their admirable attributes, but sometimes their undesirable traits can also positively influence our lives. For example, if your role model had a drinking problem, you might be inspired to limit your alcohol consumption, having learned from their mistake.

It is important to remember that role models are not perfect; they are human beings who have shortcomings like the rest of us; therefore, we must be careful to avoid being influenced by their negative behaviors. You can learn a lot from role models by emulating the qualities you admire and learning from their mistakes.

Who Is Your Role Model?

For the next activity, you will determine who has been a positive role model in your life and why you admire them. You will also consider who has negatively influenced you by encouraging you to engage in unhealthy, unsafe, dishonest, or illegal activities. These are the people who convince you to engage in undesirable behaviors that impede your success.

WHO ARE YOUR ROLE MODELS?

 Using the chart below, determine who you model your life after and why you chose this person.

WHO IS YOUR ROLE MODEL?	LIST THEIR POSITIVE TRAITS	LIST THEIR NEGATIVE BEHAVIORS

How Sensory Preferences Affect Career Choices

The next activity will help you reflect on how sensory preferences influence your career choices. Do you prefer a quiet environment with little social interaction or a career that allows you to interact with many people in a bustling environment? Consider what you have learned about your sensory likes and dislikes when choosing your profession along with the following:

1. Do you prefer working for a large company that provides opportunities for advancement and job security?

2. Do you prefer working for a small company where you know most of the employees and possibly have more diverse responsibilities?

3. Do you prefer to be a self-employed business owner who accepts full-time responsibility for all aspects of running the business, including developing a workforce and ensuring the success of the business?

You should also consider if you enjoy:

- Working with other people or working independently

- Seeing daily quantitative results or enjoy long-term projects.

- Having a fixed schedule or one that fluctuates.

- Working at one location, multiple locations, or traveling.

- Working the day, evening, or overnight shift.

- Working weekends or holidays.

- Opportunities to transfer.

CAREER PATH ASSESSMENT

 Complete the following assessment to identify career choices that correspond to your sensory preferences.

What is your dream job and why is it your dream job?	
How demanding is this job physically, emotionally, and cognitively?	
What skills would you need to develop for this job?	
What steps would you need to take to prepare for this job?	
Is this a job that you will be able to do as you get older?	
When and how do you plan to retire from this dream job?	
What do you like and dislike about your current job?	

PROFESSIONAL DEVELOPMENT

 Professional qualities are essential for success. The following activity identifies your strengths and the professional traits that need further development.

HOW OFTEN DO YOU DISPLAY THESE PROFESSIONAL BEHAVIORS?	MORE THAN 50% OF THE TIME.	LESS THAN 50% OF THE TIME. Requires further development.
Professional Appearance Language, hygiene, clothing, and display self-confidence.		
Ethics Value honesty and professionalism.		
Dependability Arrive on time, follows through on commitments.		
Flexibility Ability to adapt to changes in a positive manner.		
Organizational Skills Efficiently plan, organize, and prioritize tasks, and manage time efficiently		
Communication Skills Professional, tactful, written, verbal, and listening skills. Communicate ideas clearly and concisely.		
Detail Oriented Pay attention to every detail.		
Motivated Self-starter. Take initiative to learn and develop new skills.		
Decision Making and Problem-Solving Skills Ability to identify problems and use critical thinking to render decisions.		
Team Player Demonstrate consideration and ability to work with others. Demonstrate the ability to support co-workers.		
Teachable Seek and appreciate instruction and feedback. Accept constructive criticism.		

SENSE OF COMMUNITY

Everyone wants to be liked by their peers and included in social gatherings. The fear of being rejected nurtures social anxiety, and anxiety impedes a person's ability to establish relationships.

All too often, people assume that likability is a special gift reserved only for the lucky few. The assumption that likability is a natural trait bestowed at birth is a fallacy. Everyone can cultivate the qualities that make a person likable. These traits are learned behaviors that are governed by our inner senses. It is never too late to develop social awareness and communication skills that make a person more likable and socially accepted.

In this session, you will complete a therapeutic exercise that allows you to evaluate your social communication competence. This assessment helps increase your self-awareness and social engagement by identifying skills that need further development.

SESSION GOALS:

☐ Complete the *Science of Social Interactions* assessment to learn about effective social communication, which requires the support of our inner senses. The interoceptive system helps us to detect gestures and how they compare to social norms. This activity will help cultivate your social skills and identify areas that require further development.

☐ Complete the *Sense of Community* worksheet to help you identify and organize your supportive network.

Please visit **http://www.SensoryAuthority.com/reader-bonus** to download additional copies of the therapeutic exercises contained in this book.

Social Acceptance

Social exclusion tops the list of things people fear most. These fears include rejection, ridicule, missing out, and loneliness. The belief that other people are enjoying a more fulfilling social life only fuels these fears. People believe that their peers have more friends and attend more social events than they do. Social psychology reports that this distorted thinking is not accurate and that false perceptions fuel anxiety and depression.

Embellished depictions on social media only add to this dilemma like the meme where a distraught young woman is sitting in her room sobbing. She wipes away her tears and flashes a big smile to take a selfie. She then starts crying again as she posts the image on social media. This illustrates that people are unhappy, but they post misleading pictures on social media, hoping to be accepted by others. The fear that causes them to embellish their lives is a form of social anxiety.

Social anxiety affects each person differently. Some people feel anxious in large crowds or meeting new people. Other people experience it when talking on the phone or ordering food at a restaurant. Stage fright is also a type of social anxiety. It is fueled by the fear of social perceptions and rejections.

Today, more and more people are suffering from social anxiety. It impacts their ability to function in society, and the fear that comes from not knowing what to say or do in social settings contributes to this problem. Although social skills seem to come naturally to some people, most people need to learn the intricacies of social engagement.

The following therapeutic activity identifies the interpersonal skills that are required for social communication. It teaches you the aspects of good communication and allows you to assess your proficiency in each area.

Social Skills Assessment

Good interpersonal skills are the foundation of social and professional relationships. They include the ability to express yourself verbally and non-verbally and to listen effectively. These skills help us to develop lasting relationships.

Research indicates effective communication is the result of the following:

- 50 % Body language, movement, and eye contact

- 45 % Tone, inflection, and other voice components

- 5 % Spoken word

Self-awareness is a pre-requisite for social awareness. The Life Changers Sensory Solutions Program increases your awareness of sensory perceptions. This awareness will increase your self-confidence and reduce your anxiety in social settings.

The first step in social skills development is assessing what skills a person has and what skills need further development. This reveals the areas of social communication that require refinement. As you complete the Social Skills Assessment, you will learn about the intricacies of social communication while evaluating your own skills in each area.

VERBAL COMMUNICATION SKILLS

The ability to initiate, respond or sustain a conversation using spoken language.

DO YOU...	ALWAYS	SOMETIMES	NEVER
Initiate a conversation			
Respond appropriately			
Use proper tone, volume, pacing, words, and phrases			
Speak clearly by articulating words			
Refrain from rambling			
Remain on topic and find common interests			
Ask open-ended questions			

EXPRESSIVE COMMUNICATION SKILLS

The ability to express ideas, thoughts, feelings, requests, and state an objection.

ARE YOU ABLE TO...	ALWAYS	SOMETIMES	NEVER
Express your feelings or opinions			
Ask a question or for clarification			
Make a request: Ex. Place an order, ask for help			
Give instructions or directions			
Give a compliment, advice, or apology			
Disagree without judgment			

Refusing a Request

Refusing a request is often more difficult than making a request. Requests made by others often include needing your time, money, talents, connections, or assistance.

3 Reasons we often do not refuse a request:

1. Fear of hurting others
2. To avoid conflict
3. Perception of being self-centered

A simple way to refuse a request is to listen to the request, then wait silently for 3 seconds as if you are considering it. You then reply, "I'm sorry, but I can't."

ARE YOU ABLE TO SAY "NO" TO …	ALWAYS	SOMETIMES	NEVER
Value conflicts: (Firmly) " I don't drink or …"			
Suggestions: "I don't think this is right for me."			
Disagreements: "Let's agree to disagree."			
Timing not right: "Thank you, not at this time."			
Social Invitations: "I'm flattered, but I have to say no."			
General Requests: "I wish I could, but it's impossible."			

RECEPTIVE LANGUAGE SKILLS

The ability to understand words, sentences, and the meaning of what others are saying.

CAN YOU…	ALWAYS	SOMETIMES	NEVER
Understand verbal instructions			
Understand and respond accurately to questions			
Interpret a blank stare or confused look			
Limit misinterpretation and the need for repeating			
Get cues by what others are doing			
Understand humor or when someone is joking			

NON-VERBAL COMMUNICATION SKILLS

This is the most powerful form of communication:
your posture, body gestures, facial expressions,
eye contact, and body movement.

DO YOU...	ALWAYS	SOMETIMES	NEVER
Maintain eye contact			
Display appropriate facial expression			
Display appropriate posture and personal space			
Display appropriate body gestures like nodding head			
Display a relaxed and calm demeanor			
Remain attentive, not distracted			

PHYSICAL BEHAVIOR

The secret of body language is your posture, body movements, and gestures.
Body language conveys a message to the other person, just like words.

DO YOU...	ALWAYS	SOMETIMES	NEVER
Stand tall, neutral head position and shoulders straight			
Keep arms in a relaxed position			
Stand still without rocking or swaying			
Avoid appearing restless or agitated			
Avoid exhibiting self-soothing behaviors (Nail-biting, scratching, rubbing, or shifting)			
Avoid yawning excessively			

LISTENING SKILLS

The ability to focus, concentrate, and to receive and interpret verbal and non-verbal messages.

DO YOU...	ALWAYS	SOMETIMES	NEVER
Provide verbal prompts like "Go on"			
Avoid interrupting or talking over others			
Avoid changing the subject inappropriately			
Provide equal time for everyone to speak			
Screen out distractions			
Picture what the speaker is attempting to communicate			

SOCIAL AWARENESS SKILLS

The ability to detect and understand what others are feeling through their actions and words.

DO YOU NOTICE...	ALWAYS	SOMETIMES	NEVER
When others look at their phone or look away			
Forced or no laughter in response to jokes			
When others squint their eyes and tilt their head			
If a person appears tense or anxious			
If a person interrupts or changes subject			
If a person makes eye contact, nods, and smiles			

FRIENDSHIP

Emotions or conduct between friends.

REQUIRED SKILL: DO YOU...	ALWAYS	SOMETIMES	NEVER
Understand different levels of friendships: Acquaintance, close friend, confidant			
Identify the characteristic of a friend: truthful, trustworthy, respectful, considerate			
Identify appropriate and inappropriate questions when developing friendships			
Respect other people's opinions, values, and point of view			
Respect cultural differences and values			

SOCIAL INTERACTIONS

An exchange between two or more individuals.

DO YOU...	ALWAYS	SOMETIMES	NEVER
Accept and give constructive criticism			
Accept responsibility and apologize if you were wrong			
Use proper communication style for the situation: formal, informal, professional			
Join conversations appropriately			
Understand the difference between personal and public information			
Admit not knowing information or topic			
Disagree with others appropriately			

SELF-REGULATION
Restricting or controlling behaviors.

DO YOU...	ALWAYS	SOMETIMES	NEVER
Use acceptable ways to express frustration or anger			
Request a break when frustrated			
Cope with being left out of a group activity			
Cope with teasing or joking comments			
Accept losing a game with becoming angry or upset			
Act appropriately when winning			
Accept making mistakes without becoming upset			
Ignore situations when appropriate to do so			
Accept change in routine			
Persevere when something is difficult			

GROUP ACTIVITIES
Several people working towards the same or similar goal.

DO YOU...	ALWAYS	SOMETIMES	NEVER
Willingly participate in groups			
Use appropriate attention-seeking behavior in a group setting			
Remain with your group			
Follow the group routine			
Work to include others in group			

Upon completion of this exercise, you should have a better understanding of the skills required for effective social communication. You should have also identified the skills that you have mastered and those that need development. This will empower you to make subtle changes to improve your communication aptitude.

You may have recognized that your sensory preferences impact some of these social skills. If you avoid sounds, you may limit verbal exchanges, and if you are under-sensitive to visual inputs, you may stand too close to others or fail to see facial expressions. Reflecting on your sensory profile will allow you to see the correlation between your sensory processing patterns and social engagement.

Likability

Why are some people more likable than others? Likable people are genuine and unpretentious. They possess a healthy balance of confidence and humility that makes them relatable. Relatability and commonalities are the foundation for social connections. We bond with people who share our interests and values.

We connect with individuals who are genuine and greet us with a sincere smile. We feel important when people give us their full attention and ask meaningful questions. Likable people are not easily distracted. They do not look at their cell phones or turn away when others speak because they understand that this diminishes a person's self-worth. Therefore, if you want to be likable, you must display a sincere interest in people's lives. You want to make them feel respected and valuable by giving them your full attention.

POINT TO PONDER...

People are like mirrors; if we look in a mirror and like what we see, we will go back several more times to admire our appearance. If we dislike what we see, we avoid that mirror. This is how we react when we meet someone. If they make us feel good about ourselves, we want to spend more time with them. If they try to outsmart, demean, or devalue us, we will avoid them.

Life-Changing Moment...

WE WITHER

The other morning, I was watching Joyce Meyer's broadcast on TV. She used a compelling illustration to make an important point. At the start of her show, she held up a beautiful rose. It was healthy and vibrant. She then placed it on the podium as she shared her lesson.

Joyce spoke about the importance of being connected to a group that nurtures our value and self-worth. She explained that we need the support of others to grow and thrive. After she shared this important message, she again held up the rose. In that short amount of time, the rose had started to wither. It was no longer connected to the bush that gave it life, so it faded away.

This illustration represents our lives and the importance of being part of a broader community. We need to be nurtured by the love and support of other people because if we try to go through life alone, we wither, just like the rose.

I wonder how many of you reading this book today have cut ties with your supportive communities. It is easy to do when you are not feeling good about yourself. Many people try to isolate themselves by taking online classes or working from home. They also do not join churches, gyms, or participate in social gatherings. Many get food delivered and do their banking from home so they can eliminate social encounters. Sadly, the technology that was meant to make our lives easier has perpetuated the loneliness and depression that is plaguing our nation. It has fostered a cycle of despair.

When people are feeling down, they tend to withdraw. This isolation feeds anxiety and low self-esteem. It also leads to depression. This substantiates the importance of being connected to a broader community: one that shares your values and beliefs.

You can find the community that is right for you by reviewing your *Interests and Hobbies* checklist. This will help you find people who share similar interests, people with whom you have things in common. This connection to others will increase your self-worth and bring meaning to your life, so you can flourish and thrive.

Sense of Community

We all know the saying, 'No man is an island,' meaning, we need each other. We rely on others' advice and support to succeed, but it is also crucial to recognize that we need to be needed. We do not only prosper from receiving love, support, and advice; we also flourish when we give it. We feel valuable and purposeful when other people need us because it brings meaning to our lives.

For the next activity, you are asked to identify the people and organizations that make up your community. These names and numbers are an invaluable resource. Although you may have already stored these numbers on your phone, I encourage you to organize them on these templates to fully appreciate your support network.

YOUR COMMUNITY

It is not easy to manage life without the help and support of others. For this exercise, you will document the names and numbers of people you can call for advice, encouragement, or support. These are the people who are vital for your success.

Mentors, Sponsors and Teachers

NAME	PHONE NUMBER

Family and Friends: People Who Care About You

NAME	PHONE NUMBER

Confidants: People Who Listen and Who You Can Trust

NAME	PHONE NUMBER

Spiritual Resources: People or Organizations Providing Spiritual Support

NAME	PHONE NUMBER

Supportive Resources: Centers, Groups, Public Services & Online Communities

NAME	PHONE NUMBER

Healthcare: Doctors, Therapists, Service Providers

NAME	PHONE NUMBER

Financial Resources: Financial Assistance or Guidance

NAME	PHONE NUMBER

SENSE OF WELL-BEING

In this session, you will learn about the eight dimensions of wellness and how they contribute to our sense of well-being. Many have been discussed in previous sessions, but it is vital that we maintain a balance in each area to minimize stress. The following therapeutic activities will help you toward achieving that goal.

SESSION GOALS:

☐ Review the Science of a Healthy Lifestyle and the eight dimensions of well-being.

☐ Complete the *Lifestyle Assessment* to determine if you are successfully maintaining your physical health.

☐ Review the Science of Relationships and how broken hearts increase stress.

☐ Complete the letter-writing activity by writing a letter you will never send to someone who left you wounded.

> Please visit **http://www.SensoryAuthority.com/reader-bonus** to download additional copies of the therapeutic exercises contained in this book.

Life-Changing Moment...

SENSE OF UNCERTAINTY

In practice, I worked with a 14-year-old girl who suffered from anxiety. Her mother said that her daughter excelled in school, but she experienced emotional outbursts throughout the day. When asked what sparked her reaction, she would yell, 'Everything.'

She was a friendly girl, though she did not have many friends. Her behaviors would scare other kids away. It was challenging to find the root cause of her problem. Then her parents shared a story about an incident that happened while attending her youth group, and it helped to divulge part of the problem.

The youth group had volunteered to do some work around the church. Their daughter was assigned a task and happily completed her work. When everyone finished their work, the youth pastor had a surprise for them. He set up a party in the rec hall, complete with food, music, and games.

The children were thrilled, excitedly running here and there, but when their daughter entered the room, she started crying and continued crying throughout the party. This confused everyone. It was the same children celebrating in the same church she had attended for years. Her reaction was perplexing.

I discussed this event with her during our session. First, I questioned if it was too loud or bright at the party, to which she replied, 'No.' I then asked her if she liked having responsibilities and receiving instructions on what to do when she was working around the church, and she answered, 'Yes.' I then asked her why she cried at the party. She started crying, saying, "No one told me there was going to be a party. I wasn't prepared, and I didn't know what I was supposed to do."

How Uncertainty Contributes to Anxiety

This young teenager cried that day because she was overwhelmed by the stress created by uncertainty. This is not uncommon. Many people like to know where they are going so they can prepare themselves accordingly. Cognitive flexibility is regulated by the interoceptive system.

Therefore, a person can display symptoms of under- or over-sensitivity.

I wondered if this incident would shed light on what triggered her stress in school. We reviewed her time analysis, evaluating the highlighted sections to determine the cause of her behaviors. It revealed that sounds triggered stress, and that uncertainty caused her meltdowns. She would have an emotional outburst when she was unsure of what to do. She would even become upset by minor changes in plans because she had not prepared for this new activity.

Understandably, her inability to adapt to change frustrated her parents and teachers. However, I assure you, it was most disturbing for her. This girl was suffering from the pain of anxiety. The uncertainty caused her to feel scared, nervous, and sick.

We have all experienced this type of anxiety at one point in our lives, like when a relationship abruptly ended, or we lost our job without warning. If we had been prepared for these changes, it would have helped us to manage them. This is why people must understand how uncertainty affects the brain and why this program is designed to prepare you for situations by teaching you how to identify possible stressors.

Sense of Well-Being

Every person's definition of well-being is based on their values and expectations. Typically, well-being or wellness means that our needs are being met in the following significant areas of our life:

Physical Wellness: Maintaining an active lifestyle, healthy diet, and sleep routine.

Social Well-being: Communicates well with others to establish healthy relationships and develop a sense of community.

Emotional Well-being: Expresses feelings, identify strengths, and feels content.

Spiritual Well-being: The ability to establish beliefs and represent them through actions to foster meaning and purpose in our lives.

Occupational Well-being: Identifies and participates in meaningful employment and rewarding hobbies.

Environmental Well-being: Lives in a safe environment that has resources to provide for daily needs.

Financial Well-being: Maintains an enjoyable lifestyle while remaining in budget.

Intellectual Well-being: Continually expands knowledge and skills.

A sense of well-being is achieved by developing a plan to realize success in every area of our lives. The following supplemental activities provide outlines to help you address the dimensions of well-being not previously discussed. As you near the end of this program, I encourage you to finish this journey with the same enthusiasm for which you began to enjoy the stress-free life you deserve.

Science of
A Healthy Lifestyle

Physical activity has been shown to be as effective as prescription drugs for reducing mild to moderate anxiety and depression. It also boosts self-confidence and helps reduce fatigue, heart disease, and many other health conditions. The following activity encourages you to evaluate your current lifestyle to identify areas that need to be refined to achieve a healthy lifestyle.

LIFESTYLE ASSESSMENT

 Complete the chart, assessing your current lifestyle. Read and answer the following questions to identify barriers that hinder progress in these areas.

LIFESTYLE ASSESSMENT	NEVER	OCCASIONALLY	MORE THAN 50% OF THE TIME
I smoke cigarettes or cigars.			
I drink alcohol.			
I take vitamins.			
I sleep 7 to 8 hours per night.			
I take medicines prescribed by my doctor.			
I maintain a healthy weight for my height.			
I exercise for at least 20 minutes each day.			
I engage in weight-bearing exercises.			
I limit my sugar intake.			
I limit the consumption of processed foods.			
I consume 2-4 servings of fresh fruits per day.			
I consume 3-5 servings of fresh vegetables per day.			
I monitor my intake of fats.			
I monitor my intake of carbohydrates.			
I consume 2-3 servings of dairy each day.			

1. What factors prevent you from maintaining a healthy diet? Is it a lack of time, money, or resources? Could it be that you do not know how to prepare healthy foods, or is it a lack of motivation?

_____

_____

2. What prevents you from exercising regularly? Is it a lack of time, money, or resources? Is it that you do not know how to plan and implement a safe, effective exercise routine, or do you lack the motivation to exercise?

_____

_____

3. Would you like to adopt a healthy lifestyle? If so, when would you like to start this lifestyle change?

_____

_____

4. Identify barriers that prohibit you from achieving this goal.

_____

_____

_____

5. Devise a plan to overcome the obstacles you identified in this activity.

BARRIERS	RESOURCES NEEDED

Life-Changing Moment...

A LETTER YOU WILL NEVER SEND

Years ago, I met a woman who was a therapist. I was not in healthcare at that time, but I found my conversation with her intriguing. I mentioned that I had recently gone through a break-up, and she asked me how I was doing. I said I was hurt because the break-up was unexpected, and I had no sense of closure.

She told me that clients often come to see her to learn how to recover from a failed relationship. So, I asked, "How does one heal from a broken heart?" She said that I needed to write the person a letter that I will never send. This letter should express how I feel and ask questions that were left unanswered. She said, "You will be surprised by how much this helps."

I didn't have to wait to write that letter to be surprised; I was already surprised that writing a letter was her solution. I even joked with her about it. She smiled and said that people expect complex answers to remedy life's complicated situations, but simple solutions are sometimes more effective. I smiled and said that I would try it, although I did not really believe that it would help me.

About a week later, with the pain from that break-up still heavy on my mind, I decided to write a letter that I would never send. In the letter, I shared my feelings, and I asked the questions that were left unanswered. I ended the letter with a heartfelt message.

To my shock and surprise, the sadness had started to dissipate, freeing my mind to think about other things. I would not have believed it was possible, but truthfully, that break-up never had the same effect on me after writing the letter.

I wondered how and why this simple act alleviated the pain of a broken relationship. It was not until years later that I learned the importance of unburdening the mind through talk therapy, art therapy, journaling, or other creative expressions. When we express feelings instead of ruminating them, the burden is lifted.

Today, I now recommend that people should write a letter that they will never send. Sometimes the letter is to a parent, spouse, or friend who caused us heartache. And of course, I recommend it to heal a broken heart because I know from experience that it works.

The Science Behind Relationships

Everyone longs to find acceptance and companionship. We all need people who care for and support us. Our desire to be loved is what fuels our longing to find romance and ever-lasting love. This desire has a powerful impact on our actions and well-being.

Love and passion cause us to do things that we never thought possible. Romantic love is a compelling motivator. It can encourage us to excel and achieve success, and it can even persuade us to go against our values and beliefs. Being in love with someone is intoxicating. It affects our ability to maintain a realistic perspective in situations. This is the reason that relationships and broken hearts are so hard to overcome.

Surveys found that being in a healthy, romantic relationship is listed as a top priority in life. Love eliminates loneliness, which is one of the top fears. Love is also inspiring; it encourages people to be the best versions of themselves, and love is satisfying, not only emotionally, but also physically. It nourishes our need to touch and be touched. It makes perfect sense that a lack of romantic love causes stress.

Unfortunately, our inability to secure a loving relationship can make us feel unlovable or inadequate. It can also feed our fear of loneliness, leaving us starved for affection. A broken heart from a failed relationship intensifies this feeling. It not only isolation that makes the situation so hard; it is also having love that has nowhere to go. So how does a person overcome the pain of a broken or lonely heart?

People have reported that opportunities to give of their time, self, and resources can help reduce this stress. When we give, we feel good about ourselves. These opportunities also provide us with a sense of purpose. Donating one's time and resources can also help sustain people who feel unfulfilled in an unhappy relationship. These acts of kindness nurture our sense of compassion, relevance, importance, and self-worth. And of course, another way to help mend a broken heart is to write a letter to the person who hurt you. Express your feelings, including the whys and the what-ifs. You will never send this letter, but I assure you, this therapeutic exercise provides significant healing.

POINT TO PONDER...

One day, I heard a radio host who used a tree analogy to describe friendships. She explained that some friends are like leaves. They remain part of the tree until the season changes, and then they are gone. Others are like the branches. They seem reliable and trustworthy, but they may not be as sturdy as you think. They might break away during difficult times. Lastly, some friends are like the root of the tree. They are securely planted in your life and support you in good and bad times.

I have always heard it said that people come into your life for a reason, a season, or a lifetime. No matter how you characterize it, I think it is important to recognize that not all friendships are meant to last a lifetime, but the ones that do last are more precious than gold.

SENSE OF PURPOSE

In this final session of the program, we discuss the importance of having a purpose greater than ourselves. This includes the significance of spirituality and of fulfilling a calling in life.

We will also examine the importance of embarking on a mission to make the world a better place than the way we found it.

SESSION GOALS:

☐ Review the importance of spirituality in managing stress and establishing purpose in your life.

☐ Identify your spiritual beliefs and how they guide your actions.

☐ Discover the importance of committing to a mission that betters society.

☐ Discover the emotional, mental, and physical benefits of giving.

Spirituality

Spirituality means different things to different people. To some, it refers to their religious beliefs. To others, spirituality is their connection to nature. Spirituality finds its roots in connecting with something or someone greater than humanity. This connection is important. It reminds us there is a higher purpose, which gives meaning to our lives and bonds us with others who share similar beliefs.

Faith in a higher being provides purpose, hope, and peace. It calms our fears by letting us know that we are not alone. Faith also comforts, guides, and directs us toward the calling for which we created. Throughout this book, I have candidly shared aspects of my faith. My faith has sustained me through many of life's hardships, and I am not sure where I would be today if I did not have a relationship with God. I am honored and humbled to say that Jesus Christ is my Lord and Savior. He has taught me that love never fails and that we should always treat others with kindness, compassion, and understanding.

I hope you understand how important it is for you to determine what you believe about the existence of a higher being. Once you establish your beliefs, you can nurture your spirituality through instruction, meditation, and prayer. You can also meet with like-minded people, fostering friendships and a sense of community. Most importantly, your faith will renew your strength and give you peace, providing the foundation that is necessary to enjoy a stress-free life.

Life-Changing Moment...

SOMEBODY'S ANGEL

Several years ago, a local family lost everything they owned in a house fire. Most of us cannot imagine what it must be like to lose all our possessions. It is devastating and frightening. Weeks later, another family went through a different kind of life-changing tragedy. These events inspired me to launch a non-profit organization called Somebody's Angel.

The premise of this outreach was to allow 'somebody' to be an 'angel' to 'somebody' in need. The people who received help felt comforted by the support of their local 'angels,' and those who donated felt fulfilled. This charitable outreach impacted lives in more ways than I thought possible.

The organization was later expanded to include Somebody's Soldier. This division supported military personnel serving abroad by donating supplies and words of support. I also wanted children to experience the joy of giving, so I introduced a new division called Somebody's Chair.

Each year around Thanksgiving, Somebody's Chair would place an empty chair in each classroom in local schools. This chair served to remind the children that 'somebody' sits before an empty table at mealtimes. The students were encouraged to bring non-perishable items to fill the empty chair. These items would be collected and donated to local food pantries.

I had hoped that we would collect a significant amount of food, but when my son Jared and I arrived with a van to pick-up the donations, our eyes filled with tears. Each school had collected hundreds of bags of food. There were bags everywhere! So much so that we needed a trailer to collect all of them.

More heartwarming were the stories the teachers shared about the giving experience. They said that children donated their snacks, their desserts from lunch, and some carried in full bags of groceries. We were also told that some children wept as they approached the chair. Their tender acts of kindness collected enough food to stock the food pantry through the new year.

Somebody's Angel was founded to help supply resources to people in need, but I soon realized that it helped the people who gave as much as those who received. It also fostered a sense of unity and gave people a sense of purpose.

The Benefits of Giving

Quite often, we are so concerned with our own needs that we fail to recognize the benefits of giving. Giving makes us feel good about ourselves. It builds our self-esteem and reduces our stress. We all have something to offer. We can give our time, attention, finances, talents, love, help, and advice, but we need only provide a little to reap the benefits of generosity.

Researchers have found that brain activity changes when we give. They found that giving stimulates the reward system in the brain, releasing endorphins and dopamine. These are the chemicals that make us feel euphoric, empowered, and happy. They also found that giving promotes healing; therefore, we can conclude that giving will help us emotionally, mentally, and physically.

Our motivation behind our giving also influences its benefits. If we give voluntarily, we enjoy more benefits than if we feel obligated to give. However, even when people felt compelled to give, they still produced feel-good chemicals in the brain.

Many people want to give, but they are unsure of how to help. I assure you, there are more options to give than you ever thought possible. Some organizations need volunteers to build swing sets or paint bedrooms for children with cancer. Many are looking for volunteers to help the elderly or people who are ill, while some groups need help to care for animals, preserve the environment, or mentor young people.

If you are interested in giving your time or resources, I encourage you to seek out opportunities in your area. Choose a cause that is important to you and contact local agencies to learn how you can help. The benefits will surely be life changing.

Life-Changing Moment...

HOW DOES THIS STORY END?

It has been my pleasure to share with you the amazing power of your senses. For years, I have witnessed how sensory awareness has changed people's lives, and I am confident that you now have the tools you need to overcome your anxiety. You developed an extensive list of sensory strategies to help you feel calm when you are upset and energized when you are tired. You also developed the insight to recognize sensory events that contribute to stress so you can control or avoid them.

I trust that this education has empowered you to enjoy a more fulfilling, purposeful life. You now understand how sensory encounters affect your behavior, relationships, decisions, and interests. You have also gained insight into how your sensory preferences impact your communication skills, sleep routine, and time management. And by completing this program, you developed a better sense of self by delineating your values, role models, and spiritual beliefs.

Now, as this book comes to an end, I hope you realize that the story of your incredible, new life is only beginning. You have the tools and knowledge you need to manage life's many stressors, and I encourage you to continue your life-changing journey by visiting me at www.sensoryauthority.com. There you will find invaluable resources, including articles, services, sensory products, and training videos to help you maintain a happy, stress-free life.

SELECT REFERENCES

Abraham, Heffron, Braley, and Lauren Drobnjiak. *Sensory Processing 101. First Printing, 2015.*

Ayres, A. Jean. *Sensory Integration and the Child: Understanding Hidden Sensory Challenges, 25th Anniversary Edition.* Los Angeles: Western Psychological Services, 2005.

Bialer, D. S. and Miller, L. J. *No Longer a Secret: Unique Common-Sense Strategies for Children with Sensory or Motor Challenges.* Arlington, TX: Sensory World, 2011.

Biel, Lindsey, and Nancy Peske. *Raising a Sensory Smart Child: The Definitive Handbook for Helping Your Child with Sensory Processing Issues.* New York: Penguin, 2009.

Craig, A.D. *How Do You Feel? An Intercoeptive Moment with your Neurogbiological Self.*

Princeton, NJ: Princeton University Press, 2014.

DiSallvo, David. "Chew Yourself A better Brain." *Forbes*, March 8, 2012

Dunn, Winnie. *Living Sensationally: Understanding Your Senses.* Philadelphia: Jessica Kingsley Publishers, 2008.

Greene, R. W. *The Explosive Child.* New York, NY: HarperCollins Publishers, 2005.

Grandin, Temple. *Temple Talks…About Autism and Sensory Issues.* Arlington, TX: Sensory World. 2015

Heller, Sharon. *Too Loud, Too Bright, Too Tight: What to do if you are Sensory Defensive in an Over-stimulating World.* New York, NY: Harper Collins, 2002.

Jemkinson, Hyde, & Saffia Ahmad. *Building Blocks For Learning: Occupational Therapy Approaches,* West Sussex, UK: John Wiley & Sons, 2008.

Kranowitz, Carol Stock. *The Out-of–Sync Child: Recognizing and Coping with Sensory Processing Disorder.* New York, NY: Penguin Group, 2005.

Kuypers, Leah, M. *The Zones of Regulation: A Curriculum Designed to Foster Self-regulation and Emotional Control.* Santa Clara: Think Social, 2011.

Lombard, Annemarie. *Sensory Intelligence: Why it Matters More than IQ and EQ.* South Africa: Metz Press, 2014.

Mahler, Kelly. *Interoception: The Eighth Sensory System.* Kansas: AAPC, 2017.

Mauro, Terri. *The Everything Parent's Guide to Sensory Processing Disorder.* Massachusetts: F & W Media, Inc., 2014.

Miller, Lucy Jane. *Sensational Kids: Hope and Help for Children with Sensory Processing Disorder.* New York: G. P. Putmans's Sons, 2006.

Minich, D. "Chew Your Food For Brain Health." Last Modified July 31, 2017. https://www.deannaminich.com/chew-your-food-for-brain-health/

Moore, Karen. *The Sensory Connection Program.* Farmingdale, MA: Therapro Inc., 2005

Smith, K. A. and Grouze, K.R., *The Sensory-Sensitive Child. Practical Solutions for Out-of-Bounds Behavior.* New York: William Morrow, 2005.

Williams, M.S. and Shellenberger, S. *How Does Your Engine Run? A Leaders Guide to the Alert Program for Self-Regulation.* Albuquerque, NM: TherapyWorks, Inc.